CREATIVE THERAPIES IN PRACTICE

The *Creative Therapies in Practice* series, edited by Paul Wilkins, introduces and explores a range of arts therapies, providing trainees and practitioners alike with a comprehensive overview of theory and practice. Drawing on case material to demonstrate the methods and techniques involved, the books are lively and informative introductions to using the creative arts in therapeutic practice.

Books in the series:

Psychodrama
Paul Wilkins

Dance Movement Therapy
Bonnie Meekums

Music Therapy
Rachel Darnley-Smith and Helen M. Patey

MUSIC THERAPY

Rachel Darnley-Smith
and
Helen M. Patey

 SAGE Publications
London • Thousand Oaks • New Delhi

ISBN 0-7619-5776-8 (hbk)
ISBN 0-7619-5777-4 (pbk)
© Rachel Darnley-Smith and Helen M.Patey 2003
First published 2003
Reprinted 2004

SAGE Publications Ltd
1 Oliver's Yard
33 City Road
London EC1Y 1SP

SAGE Publications Inc
2455 Teller Road
Thousand Oaks
California 91320

SAGE Publications India Pvt Ltd
B–42 Panchsheel Enclave
PO Box 4109
New Delhi 110 017

British Library Cataloguing in Publication data

A catalogue record for this book is available from the British Library

Library of Congress Control Number: 2002107098

Typeset by C&M Digitals Pvt. Ltd., Chennai, India
Printed digitally and bound in Great Britain by
TJ International Ltd.., Padstow, Cornwall

For our parents

CONTENTS

FOREWORD

More than half a century on from the acknowledged beginning of the present day profession of music therapy, there should be a sense of confidence, pride and achievement in the developments that have been made. Music is increasingly acknowledged as a medium of therapy – of inspiration, relaxation, motivation and integration. It is truly appropriate that the opening of this book reflects the multicultural role of music in a group experience, highlighting so vividly the barriers that can be overcome through sharing the varieties of melody and song, and yet incorporating the integration of rhythm. Music brings people together – yes, but more than that it integrates people with widely differing experiences, origins and attitudes.

The process that many believe stands at the centre of the music therapy treatment is the development of a therapeutic relationship within music that facilitates the therapy. Yet therapeutic process can, paradoxically, be seen as rather a 'chicken and egg' situation. Does a musical experience lead to the emergence of a therapeutic objective, or does a therapeutic goal define the musical experience that is required? One might consider this question in relationship to the difference between psychotherapeutic or behavioural approaches, between qualitative or quantitative investigations, process or outcome methods, terms such as 'client' and 'patient' or even between 'music as therapy' and 'music in therapy'. I believe the real truth is that the client's needs determine both the nature of the musical experience, and the direction of the therapy. Rachel Darnley-Smith and Helen Patey have given us impressive case stories that demonstrate how clients' needs really are addressed through music therapy.

This book gives a multi-faceted insight into the application of the principles of music therapy seen from both a psychoanalytical viewpoint (Analytic Music Therapy), and from the Humanistic/Anthropsophic (Nordoff-Robbins Therapy). Both authors are very experienced therapists and music therapy teachers, and they have succeeded in illustrating basic theory and professional methods with very appropriate and focused vignettes from case material. It is logically and well constructed, following a path from theory and training to clinical application. There is an essentially British character to this book, and the effective way the authors have presented a list of 'key events' in the history of music therapy in the United Kingdom is a remarkable testament to 45 years of development. The resources drawn on for this text reference Winnicott, Trevarthen, Wing, Tustin, Laing and Horden, as well as mainly British music therapists, and this gives a precise framework and context for the deeper, more complex case material in Chapters 6 to 8. These are human stories, revealing both despair and hope, pain and healing, where musical experiences in music therapy meet very specific and demanding needs.

Rachel Darnley-Smith and Helen Patey have managed so well to tell their story of music therapy offering the framework of theory, training and professional practice, and the complementary value of Analytic Music Therapy and Nordoff-Robbins Music Therapy within improvisation. The authors devote a whole chapter to promoting a wider understanding of improvisation, describing its value as a form of play, free association, with more or less structure depending on the form of intervention and the client's needs. There is really a valuable resource of meaningful and relevant examples from their own clinical work. These examples clearly validate and illustrate the seminal theoretical concept of the first great pioneer of music therapy in the United Kingdom, Juliette Alvin, who taught us that music is a creation of people, and therefore we can see people in their music.

Professor Tony Wigram PhD

Acknowledgments

Alison Levinge for her collaborative work in the early stages of this book.

The patients with whom we have worked and the co-workers who have given us their support.

Ruth Berkowitz, Sandra Brown and Helen Odell-Miller for their supervision at various stages of our professional lives.

Paul Wilkins for his astute and critical editing, together with the editorial and production staff at Sage Publications.

Pauline Etkin, Julie Sutton and Mercédès Pavlicevic, for reading early versions of chapters and their professional support. Christopher Gale, April Parkin and David Stewart for sending us accounts of the development of music therapy in the UK. Edward and Margaret Patey who gave us books and quotations, P.M. Darnley-Smith, who read the manuscript all the way through.

Lucy Browne, Heather Gaebler, Jo Joyce, Helen Moss, Sarah Tucker, who read chapters and gave invaluable comments, together with Colin Constantine, Mary T. Darnley-Smith, Christine Driver, Fran Heasman, Sarah Hoskyns, Beth York, Julienne Maclean and Diane Rollo, all of whom helped in a wide variety of ways to make this book happen.

INTRODUCTION

Shortly before beginning to write this book together, we collaborated on the provision of a music therapy summer school at Utah State University in the US. The head of the music therapy department, Dr Elizabeth York, had become interested in the improvisational methods of music therapy used in the UK and had met with us to exchange ideas and thoughts about our respective working practices. This led to the invitation to devise a summer course suitable for music therapy practitioners and students. The course aimed to introduce improvisational music therapy techniques through practical workshops and presentations of clinical material, together with a historical and theoretical background to the subject. The week of teaching was as stimulating as it was enjoyable and, following in the long tradition of trading across oceans, we found that we returned home with at least as much as we had taken to Utah. The lively interest of our group of American students had enabled us to look at the recent history of our own music therapy profession through fresh eyes, and to clarify the areas of greatest significance. The experience also provided the opportunity to view our clinical practice critically and to place music therapy in the UK in a worldwide context.

The purpose of this book is to present ideas arising from our clinical work against the backdrop of the theory and practice of music therapy that has developed in Britain since the 1950s. We will show how the present-day music therapy practice of using live, improvised music emerged out of the experience of musicians, educators and healthcare professionals and from the work of several influential pioneers.

Music therapy is potentially a vast topic, even when limiting the view to a British perspective. We need to begin by clarifying that we write from our own personal experience and that we have focused upon what we know best, our clinical work with clients of all ages.

We know from experience that to play music with another person is to invite a relationship to develop and to establish an emotional engagement. This has become our chief interest and our motivation for continuing to work as clinicians. While the use of music as the principle medium of therapy has remained central, theories and practice of analytic psychotherapy have contributed a framework of understanding that has made sense of the therapeutic process and provided us with invaluable insights. Using the ideas and knowledge which we have both absorbed through many years of working and teaching in music therapy, we hope to illustrate how we work and how we make sense of what we do.

Part I provides a background to music therapy, in Chapter 1 defining what it is and how it works, together with briefly documenting the history of the modern profession. In Chapter 2 we present two important approaches to music therapy, one psychodynamic and the other music-centred, that were developed in the UK, but are now recognised worldwide. Chapter 3 explores the role of music in music therapy and the significance of a therapeutic frame. In Chapter 4 we describe how music therapists train for the profession and outline some of the resources which enable a therapist to keep working over many years.

Part II focuses on practical and clinical issues. Chapters 5 and 7 contain ideas about working practice, taken directly from our own experience, and tackle some problematic areas. In Chapters 6 and 8, the clients take centre stage; here we present case studies that we hope will simply 'speak for themselves'. Chapter 9 guides the reader towards some practical methods of finding out more about music therapy.

In our summer course in Utah, we were asked to give clear definitions of the predominant models of music therapy in Britain. Although we were able to define the terms we used, we found ourselves reluctant to nail our own colours to one mast. Just as the pioneers of music therapy were enriched by their wide-ranging musical, philosophical and psychological experiences, we too have not only our personal histories but also the richness of influences passed on to us by our clients, teachers, supervisors and colleagues. In the pages that follow we want to convey our passion and fascination for our work, and also the profound nature of the experience which belongs to both the client and therapist.

Rachel Darnley-Smith
Helen M. Patey

PART I

Getting Started

1

In the Beginning

Ama, a woman in her twenties, sits down in a group of people she does not know and whose language she hardly speaks. There is an uncomfortable pause. John tells Paul to 'Sing us a song'. Paul takes a breath and suddenly the German words of a song by Schubert ring out. The music finishes and most of the group members convey their appreciation. Someone then suggests that John 'sings a song'. John explains to the group that he is from Ireland and immediately starts to sing a song in Gaelic, stamping his foot and accompanying himself on a small tambour. Many in the room tap their feet and some reach for percussion instruments to play with John's strident beat. His song finishes and another group member asks Ama, in her own language, if she would like to join in. After a brief conversation, she starts to sing, long melodic lines in a very high register. The group sits listening in silence until she stops. There is another pause, but this time it feels more relaxed. The group leader, a music therapist, reaches for a drum and invites everyone to join her. Soon the whole group is playing, and although there are many individual sounds and rhythms, a new piece of music is jointly created, there and then.

Music therapy is a modern profession whose practice requires skill and theoretical knowledge. It is also a vocation, involving a deep commitment to music and the desire to use it as a medium to help others. Although music therapy has only been established as a profession relatively recently, the connection between music and therapy is not new. Writers and historians have repeatedly commented upon a human preoccupation with music as part of healing and medicine, and we can find this recorded and recounted in history, myth, legend and literature over the past 2000 years. As far as we can tell, music probably existed as a form of healing in the most primitive of societies (West, 2000: 51). Today it is practised throughout the world, its effectiveness being explained by knowledge systems as diverse as magic and science.

Why might this be so? It seems appropriate to begin by speculating *why* music might be a tool for healing worldwide and why 'at various times and in various cultures over the past two and a half millennia – and probably still further back in time – music has been medicine' (Horden, 2000: 1).

Contemporary research from child psychology and psychobiology has demonstrated the innate properties of musicality (Trevarthen and Malloch, 2000). Innate musicality has a vital function from the moment we are born, when we use sound as our earliest means of communication. The sounds an infant might make in any one moment have pitch, timbre, rhythm, intensity and melody. Furthermore, these sounds communicate feelings such as hunger, contentment, the need for sleep, and so on. The infant uses these sounds to interact, and, all being well, eventually learns to talk as developmental processes take place and the sounds are extended into speech. A parent also is able to communicate instinctively with the infant, employing elements which are familiar to us through music-making, for example, turn-taking, timing and regulating the pitch and timbre of the vocalisations. So, the musicality referred to here does not imply having perfect pitch or being able to play a musical instrument to a high standard. This intuitive manipulation of musical sound has been called 'Communicative Musicality' (Trevarthen and Malloch, 2000: 5–7), which refers to 'those attributes of human communication, which are particularly exploited in music ... [and which] is vital for companionable parent/infant communication'. Research has also demonstrated that a lack of opportunity for this early communication can have a profound effect upon the emotional and cognitive development of an infant (Malloch, 1999: 157).

But sound is not only used as a means of self-expression and relationship in the first few months of life. It is well known that musical sound is part of life in many different ways and for different purposes. As music therapists have frequently commented, humans are musical beings. Our hearts beat and we move 'in time'. We speak and communicate in pitches, rhythms and timbre. Ethnomusicologist Gregory (1997) lists the main traditional uses of music which 'are common to nearly all societies': lullabies, the games of children, storytelling, work songs, dancing, music used in religious ceremonies, in festivals, in war, as a personal symbol, salesmanship, to promote ethnic or group identity, as communication within language itself, for personal enjoyment, in healing and in trance (1997: 123–37).

Music therapists are often asked to give lectures or workshops to colleagues, potential clients, students or the interested general public. In such situations it is always stimulating to invite the audience to contribute personal thoughts about their relationship to music. At these moments the energy in the room seems to surge, as people begin to share their experiences, finding that in talking about music there is much common ground between them. A mother may relate an anecdote of her unborn baby responding to music in the womb. Parents frequently relate the power of their non-verbal and essentially musical relationship with a new-born child. Others will speak of listening to music at the end of a stressful day or during a car journey. Many will talk about the importance of particular music that evokes either painful or joyful memories, from a time of being bereaved, or a time of being in love. As this shows, people do not need to be told about the therapeutic qualities of music – they have frequently already experienced them in their everyday lives.

So to return to the question, why is music as a healing phenomenon not restricted to time or place? We believe it is because the elements of music are fundamental to the human condition and have the potential to be used in the pursuit of common therapeutic goals, as self-expression (individually and collectively), in communication and to enhance physical, spiritual and emotional well-being.

Let us now look at a definition of music therapy to see how these elements of music are systematically employed in the modern discipline.

What is Music Therapy?

The World Federation of Music Therapy (WFMT) defines music therapy in the following way:

> Music therapy is the use of music and/or musical elements (sound, rhythm, melody and harmony) by a qualified music therapist, with a client or group, in a process designed to facilitate and promote communication, relationships, learning, mobilization, expression, organization, and other relevant therapeutic objectives, in order to meet physical, emotional, mental, social and cognitive needs. Music therapy aims to develop potentials and/or restore functions of the individual so that he or she can achieve better intra- and interpersonal integration and consequently a better quality of life through prevention, rehabilitation or treatment. (1997: 1)

This definition is necessarily broad so that it can encompass the variety of different models and methods of practice which exist worldwide. In the international music therapy community, two distinct applications of music as therapy can be found:

- the use of music for its inherent restorative or healing qualities; and
- the use of music as a means of interaction and self-expression within a therapeutic relationship.

The Use of Music for its Inherent Restorative or Healing Qualities

Some forms of music therapy use the physical properties of music in treatment and as healing. The role of the relationship between client and therapist is in most cases secondary to the importance of the application of music as treatment. Here are some examples:

Vibroacoustic Therapy
The vibration of sounds or single tones has been used 'in past civilisations and in different cultures … as a means of treating physical disabilities and pain … and psychosomatic disorders' (Skille and Wigram 1995: 23–4). A modern version of this treatment, which makes use of the physiological effects of musical vibrations upon the body, has been developed, particularly in Scandinavia and Britain, since the 1960s. It was known in Norway initially as the 'music bath' and more recently as vibroacoustic therapy. Skille and Wigram write that:

> The music bath is trying to create an environment whereby the body is 'bathed' in sound and vibration … The equipment (patented on a worldwide basis) consists of a bed/bench or chair with several built-in loud speakers. This is connected to a signal unit with six channels containing a cassette player which can run various tapes.
> The process of vibroacoustic therapy involves lying a client on the bed so that the sound is being transferred by air directly to the body of the client. (1995: 25)

Examples of conditions which have responded well to the treatment include cerebral palsy, asthma, abdominal pain, constipation, insomnia, menstrual pain and sports injuries (Skille and Wigram, 1995: 38–40). Whilst essentially a receptive technique of music therapy, Hooper (2001: 75) discusses the interpersonal involvement required of the therapist, and also cites how vibroacoustic therapy can be used to encourage a therapeutic relationship and lead towards the client's involvement in the more active methods of music therapy prevalent in the UK.

The Use of Music-making as a Direct Means of Cure in Mental or Physical Illness

Music therapy researcher and historian Chava Sekeles describes how ancient techniques of music therapy are demonstrated today worldwide, for example by Navajo Indians, who use music as a direct means of cure. She writes 'The tribal healer is still considered to be the best diagnostic, his advice and medicines are considered to be extremely powerful, while his extranatural and supernatural powers go totally unchallenged' (1996: 6). The practice of medicine is accompanied by chants and song, over a traditional nine-day period, either performed by a specially trained singer or by the healer himself. 'The Navajo believe that singing and incantation are the central means by which harmony can be restored to both the patient's body and soul and to his surroundings' (Sekeles, 1996: 6).

The Use of Recorded Music as Therapy Supplementary to the Cure of Physical Illness

In the United States methods of music therapy have been developed where recorded pieces of music are used in the relief of pain and the reduction of pain, anxiety or stress, so that patients require fewer drugs (Standley, 1995: 3–22). One procedure involves the patient listening to their chosen music on high-quality equipment, during or immediately before medical treatment. Wherever possible the patient retains control over the volume and the stopping and starting of the music. This type of music therapy takes place within a variety of medical settings, including surgery where it is used 'pre-operatively to reduce anxiety and reduce the amount of anaesthesia required' (Standley, 1995: 12). Clients include those on kidney dialysis, where music is used to reduce discomfort and serve as a distraction, and during childbirth. Other clients in Standley's survey of passive music listening include those suffering from cancer, where music is used in the reduction of pain and to enhance the analgesic effects of medication. Passive music listening is also included in the treatment of premature or sick infants where it is used to promote weight gain and to reduce the length of hospitalisation (Standley, 1995: 12).

The Use of Music as a Means of Interaction and Self-expression Within a Therapeutic Relationship

The majority of music therapists across the world would acknowledge their use of music as a means of interaction and self-expression within a therapeutic relationship. There are, however, many different ways in which this is carried out, depending on factors such as the number of clients, the setting of the therapy, and the aims and theoretical underpinning of the work (Bruscia, 1998).

In this section we have chosen three models of treatment.

Community Music Therapy

Community Music Therapy is a psychosocial intervention, which aims to provide treatment within the community where the clients are living. The term has recently been used to describe the work undertaken by music therapists outside the boundaries of the one-to-one or small group therapy sessions. In particular, it is applied to situations where the music therapist is responding flexibly to the social and cultural context of the setting in which they work (Ansdell, 2002). This could be seen as following in the footsteps of the enlightened Victorian philanthropists who saw the importance of creating a musical community within the walls of the hospital or asylum through encouraging choirs, bands and concert performances (Tyler, 2000). In the same tradition we will see Mary Priestley's broad interpretation of music therapy in St Bernard's Hospital in the 1970s, which included open informal music sessions and performances by the therapists (see Chapter 2).

Ansdell has made a distinction between Community Music Therapy, which is undertaken by a trained State Registered Therapist, within a clinical discipline, and Community Music, which is often user-led and project orientated, although both take place within the community. Darnley-Smith, in a survey of her work in a Day Centre for people with physical disabilities, differentiated between therapeutic music-making and music therapy, although in this instance the same therapist facilitated both kinds of music. For example, playing Christmas Carols and running a classical music 'listening group' came under the heading 'therapeutic music,' while an ongoing improvisational 'music and speech group' for people with hearing loss was seen as music therapy (Darnley-Smith, 1989).

Although the term 'Community Music Therapy' is relatively new, the work it refers to has constantly been developed pragmatically by music therapists, addressing issues of culture, community and society together with needs that are personal, individual and private.

Guided Imagery and Music (GIM)

This 'in-depth psychotherapeutic method' (Goldberg, 1995: 128) of music therapy was originally devised during the 1970s by Helen Bonny, a music therapist at the Maryland Psychiatric Research Centre in the US. 'In her research, Bonny found that when subjects listened to a carefully selected programme of [taped] classical music while in a relaxed state, powerful feelings and symbolic images were evoked, leading to significant insights into therapy issues' (Goldberg, 1995: 112). For each session, the therapist chooses the programme of taped music, basing the choice upon the history of the client, a 'formulation of the therapeutic issues' and in support of the client's current mood (Goldberg, 1995: 114–5). In GIM there is a standard procedure for sessions, as devised by Bonny (Goldberg, 1995: 114): '(1) The preliminary conversation, (2) the induction (relaxation and focus), (3) The music listening phase, and (4) the post-session integration.' After the music has been played, the client is encouraged to share all 'perceptions and experiences within the music' with the therapist, who writes them down. The role of the therapist, who must be completely attuned to the client, is to 'observe, listen and verbally reflect the process, serving to encourage, help and comfort as the client moves through the experience' (Goldberg, 1995: 115). The method has been successfully applied to a variety of client groups, particularly those without specific clinical needs, who may use it as a means of self-exploration and fulfilment. Practising the method requires special training and supervision, after qualification as a music therapist.

Improvisational Music Therapy

In improvisational music therapy, live improvised music-making is used as a medium for communication between client and therapist as the focus of a 'helping relationship'. The practice of music therapy in Britain today is largely based on the use of improvised music (Wigram, Odell-Miller and Rogers, 1993: 574), and it is this approach that will be examined in the greatest depth in this book. The American music therapist and researcher Bruscia (1987) has documented many models of 'Improvisational Music Therapy'. He suggests that, in addition to having a 'fundamental philosophy regarding the nature of music therapy and the role of improvisation, each model of improvisational therapy is rooted in one or more treatment theories' (Bruscia, 1987: 10). In the UK there are two predominant theoretical stances that inform the teaching and practice of music therapy at the beginning of the twenty-first century. One approach regards the music as the primary medium through which the therapy takes place, while the other draws on the theories and practice of psychodynamic psychotherapy to inform an understanding of the therapeutic relationship, both inside and outside the music. The origins of these two approaches will be examined in detail in Chapter 2.

Towards the Modern Profession

When did the modern profession of music therapy begin and how did it develop? Gouk (2000: 3) suggests that the emergence of music therapy as 'a fully accredited profession' in the United States was marked in 1948 with the publication of *Music and Medicine*, a substantial volume of essays edited by Dorothy M. Schullian and Max Schoen. This is how the book begins:

> The tragic years of World War II witnessed an amazing growth in the interdependence of music and medicine. The growth was apparent in particular in the heightened role played by musical therapy in military hospitals and in the increasingly frequent use of industrial music in factories. But the times of stress, while they developed in higher degree methods first employed centuries ago, could reduce to no ordered whole the complicated forces acting upon one another in the fields of music and medicine, and the result in too many cases was confusion and bewilderment. (1948: vii)

We do not learn here what the 'confusion and bewilderment' was, but Schullian and Schoen compiled the volume explicitly to further understanding and scholarship and to promote the new developments in music therapy, which were already taking place in the US. These developments included the setting-up of training courses at Michigan State University in 1944, and Kansas University, Texas, in 1946, and later in 1950, the founding of the National Association of Music Therapy (Bunt, 1994: 4).

At the same time, possibly inspired by developments in the US (Alvin, 1968), new experimental activity using music as a therapeutic tool was taking place in the UK. In an anonymous article 'Pioneers in Music Therapy', published in the bulletin of the BSMT (see p. 15) (BSMT, 1968), one story exemplifies some of the work taking place in the late 1940s. An account is given of the work done by Dr Sydney Mitchell and others who had conducted research and written 'many papers' on music therapy. At Warlingham Park Hospital, Mitchell had formed an orchestra of patients 'including string players, pianists and percussion instruments' where 'the primary object was treatment rather than a high standard of performance'. He also analysed the effects of recorded music upon his patients, and whilst he found that 'classical music seemed to give a sense of security' he also found that 'the most effective means towards the harmony of a group was folk songs and traditional music based upon the most deep-seated and cosmic relationship [which] strikes a psychological chord and brings people together' (BSMT, 1968: 18). The article goes on to describe how Mitchell's colleagues at nearby hospitals also carried out experiments into music therapy:

> Drs Zanker and Glatt used live music in their research on alcoholic and neurotic patients and analysed the individual answers to the questionnaire filled in by each of the patients. Their general conclusion was that 'patients' reactions to music can be of diagnostic value as they sometimes enable the uncovering of unconscious attitudes. By helping to break down defences, fostering abreaction and bringing about emotional release music can be a therapeutic adjunct to other forms of therapy. (BSMT, 1968: 18–19)

After the death of Sidney Mitchell, his wife Nora Gruhn, who had an international career as an opera singer, continued the experimental music therapy in two of the 'mental hospitals' where Mitchell had worked, and extended it into other hospitals. This is an early example of the practice of music therapy developing out of the work of medical practitioners and transferring into the domain of musicians, for whom formal therapeutic training had not yet been devised. During the late 1950s musicians, teachers, doctors and therapists began to meet together and formed a special interest organisation, the Society for Music Therapy and Remedial Music. From this evolved the first training course, which was held at the Guildhall School of Music and Drama in 1968, directed by Juliette Alvin. It was not until 1982 that music therapy became recognised as an effective form of treatment within the National Health Service in Britain and gaining recognition had not been a swift or easy process. Music therapists needed to demonstrate that they had a serious form of treatment to offer, more specialised than, for example, the use of music as a recreational activity which had been common in hospitals for many years. Crucial to official recognition was the need to show that the therapeutic treatment had some objective purpose which supported the treatment aims of mainstream medicine or psychiatry, and that there were recognisable skills and a body of knowledge which a music therapist could acquire through training. It was not enough to be a musician who intuitively used musical skills to work with people who might be ill or otherwise in need. There had to be an aim to the therapy, an objective means of describing it, and a method through training of assessing who was sufficiently skilled to undertake it. Most important of all, music therapy needed to convince critical outsiders that it was a discipline that could survive scrutiny and detailed questioning of its methods and claims. Immediately prior to the Health Service recognition, Leslie Bunt, a music therapist who had trained with Alvin, carried out a series of research projects with children in an area of London. He writes:

> When I started out as a music therapy researcher in England in the late 1970s it soon became apparent that much clearer descriptive evidence needed to be collated in order to move on from some of the earlier, more anecdotal, albeit pioneering summaries of work with children published in the 1960s and the early to mid-1970s. There was mounting pressure from funding agencies and other professionals – especially from doctors and psychologists – to relate practice to eventual outcome and to organise descriptive evidence from within clearer operational and experimental frameworks. (1994: 109)

This echoes the test of science to which Hippocrates, his fellow physicians and students subjected themselves in fifth century BC Greece. Their concerns were not very different from those of the health care professionals of today. They wanted to lift medicine out of an unregulated world where magic, religion and science mingled together to the detriment of the development of healing cures and techniques. Hippocratic writings demonstrate the development of rigorous observation and the writing of case studies as a means of proving clinical worth. Lloyd, in his introduction to these writings, explains that:

> It was in the late sixth or early fifth century [BC] that the first sustained critical investigations into the causes and treatment of diseases began and we find the first attempts to define and defend the status of medicine as a rational discipline or *technē*. (1986: 13)

In the Hippocratic writings a critique is presented of the common practice in healing of relying upon the citation of 'divine elements', that is to say, what was unseen or subjectively felt. Divine elements might be cited both as the source of a disease, where its origin was inexplicable, and as the means through which a healer offered treatment. A bitingly cynical view of such an approach to the treatment of epilepsy provides an insight into the struggle and frustration of early Greek physicians who were seeking to establish a rational approach to their work (Lloyd, 1986: 237–8). Indeed, the work of modern music therapists in gaining statutory recognition has involved a similar process of answering questions about whether music therapy works and if so, how it works, but in such a way that incorporated subjective and intuitive processes involved in therapy. It is most unlikely that the early pioneers of modern music therapy attributed the success or failure of their treatment of patients to *divine* elements. However, they could never have established their methods without an intuitive, and in some cases spiritual, belief in the power of music to affect the lives of their children and adult clients.

Organising Music Therapy: 1960–82

The Society for Music Therapy and Remedial Music originally aimed to bring together individuals interested in music therapy and to examine how professional practice could be developed. During the early 1960s the Executive Committee consisted of music educators, psychotherapists, medical practitioners and other professionals, many of whom continued to be well-known for their work some 40 years later. They arranged short training courses (Dobbs, 1966: 7), which were designed as introductions to music therapy, with a wide variety of invited speakers. Professor Dennis Fry, Head of the Department of Phonetics, University College London, spoke about 'Sound and Psychology' (1962) while Frank Howes (1962), then music critic of *The Times*, gave a lecture entitled 'Rhythm and Man'. The courses were gradually extended until Allen Percival, then the Principal of the Guildhall School of Music and Drama, found space and teaching facilities for a full-time training course to begin in September 1967. The society changed its name to the British Society for Music Therapy (BSMT) in January of the same year, due to the 'growing international contacts and consequent desirability of avoiding confusion of identity at international gatherings with societies from other English-speaking countries with similar names' (Dobbs, 1968: 3). The breadth of international contacts at this time are exemplified by accounts in the BSMT bulletins of Alvin's trip to Japan

(Alvin, 1968: 11–25), and of the showing of the film, 'Music Therapy for the Retarded Child' which she made in the US (Johnson, 1966: 8). The BSMT has remained a charitable organisation which aims to 'promote the use and development of music therapy. It disseminates information and organises conferences, workshops and meetings. Its membership is open to all who have an interest in music therapy' (BSMT, 2000, Information Booklet).

The Association of Professional Music Therapists (APMT), formed in 1976, however, developed as a body concerned with the work and professional requirements of qualified music therapists and offering services to students. The work of the APMT has gradually broadened, as the work of music therapists has developed, but its main concerns have always been:

- Pay and working conditions
- Training
- Research, including the convening of scientific meetings and conferences
- Linking with statutory organizations such as the Department of Health, the former Council for Professions Supplementary to Medicine and its successor the Health Professions Council

Listed below are some key events in modern music therapy in the UK, adapted from various accounts of the profession's recent history: Bunt (1994: 3–16), Tyler (2000), Loth (2000), Wigram et al. (1993: 573–604), Wigram and Heal (1993), Sutton (2000), Gale (2000), Robertson (1996).

1958

- Society for Music Therapy and Remedial Music, formed by Juliette Alvin, renamed the British Society for Music Therapy (BSMT) in 1967.

1961 onwards

- Short training courses arranged by the BSMT for professionals interested in developing music therapy.

1965

- Publication of *Music Therapy for the Handicapped Child* by Juliette Alvin.

1968

- Guildhall School of Music and Drama, London. First full-time post-graduate professional training course, set up by Juliette Alvin.

1971

- Publication of *Therapy in Music for Handicapped Children and Music Therapy in Special Education* by Paul Nordoff and Clive Robbins.

1974

- Goldie Leigh Hospital, South London. First training course taught by Paul Nordoff and Clive Robbins, initiated by Sybil Beresford-Peirse. (The training course is today based at the Nordoff–Robbins Music Therapy Centre in Kentish Town, North London.)

1975

- Publication of two new texts:
  Music Therapy by Juliette Alvin.
  Music Therapy in Action by Mary Priestley.

1976

- Association of Professional Music Therapists (APMT) formed by a group of music therapists including Tony Wigram, Mary Priestley, Angela Fenwick, Esme Towse and Auriel Warwick. The first Chair was Angela Fenwick.

1977

- Death of Paul Nordoff.
- Publication of *Creative Music Therapy* by Paul Nordoff and Clive Robbins.

1978

- First music therapy post in Scotland set up by Julienne Cartwright at Herdmanflat Hospital, Haddington.

1980

- Research Fellowship set up at City University, London. Leslie Bunt appointed as first research fellow.

1981

- Southlands College (now part of Roehampton Institute) in South London. New postgraduate diploma course set up by Elaine Streeter, who had trained with Nordoff and Robbins.

1982

- Award of pay and grading structure for music and art therapists by the Department of Health and Social Security.
- Courses Liaison Committee formed by Tony Wigram to bring together the heads of the three existing music therapy training courses.
- Death of Juliette Alvin.

1983

First research conference held at City University, London. The conference demonstrated the debate, which was to be ongoing, about the use of qualitative and quantitative methods of research for music therapy (Wigram, 1993b: 138).

1985

- Leslie Bunt awarded the first degree of Doctor of Philosophy in music therapy in the UK for his research entitled 'Music Therapy and the Child with a Handicap: Evaluation of the Effects of Intervention'.
- Music therapists employed in Wales for the first time, at St Cadoc's Hospital, Caerleon, Gwent. The first post-holder was Rachel Burbridge.
- Second Research Conference held entitled 'Presentations in Music Therapy Research'. This conference continued the themes of the first in looking for suitable research methodology in music therapy, and specified 'the need for some additional

research into the musical process and client-centred research' (Wigram, 1993b: 138).

1987

- Scottish Music Therapy Council formed 'to represent APMT members in Scotland and to undertake negotiations with Scottish authorities ... To promote the development of music therapy posts, projects and training opportunities in Scotland' (SMTC Constitution, 1987). First Chair of the SMTC was Mary Troup.
- Third Research Conference. This conference included exploration of new techniques, including video sampling and also techniques which involved the clients themselves in the process of collecting data, through self-evaluation. Research was now established as a major concern for the profession, with regular conferences held.
- The BSMT and the APMT merged some of their current publications to create the first volume of the *Journal of British Music Therapy*. The first editor was Margaret Campbell.
- Belfast, Northern Ireland. Music therapist Julie Sutton began a process to establish music therapy in Northern Ireland, supported by the work of George Gibson, who had trained with Juliette Alvin in London, and Veronica Cosgriff, an Australian music therapist living in Belfast.

1988

- Music Therapy was recognised as a professional qualification by local government Social Services in England and Wales.
- First Arts Therapies (art, music, drama and dance-movement) Conference entitled 'Shared Creativity' held in Northern Ireland, run jointly by the BSMT and the Northern Ireland Group for Art as Therapy.

1989

- Inaugural meeting of the All-Wales Network Committee for Arts Therapies Professions at Aberystwyth. This was formed with the agreement of the UK professional bodies to enable the four arts therapies professions (see above) to have a visible presence in

Wales, and to promote links between arts therapists across the Principality. Chris Gale was the first convenor.

1990

- Supervision formally recognised by the APMT as integral to clinical practice.
- Northern Ireland Music Therapy Trust founded and spearheaded by Dr Michael Swallow, a consultant neurologist based in Belfast.
- Scottish Music Therapy Trust set up to receive donations to support music therapy in Scotland.

1991

- Bristol University. First part-time postgraduate diploma in music therapy course set up by Leslie Bunt. This course broadened the entry requirements to include applicants from non-classical music backgrounds.
- State Registration applied for by Tony Wigram on behalf of the membership of the APMT. Chair: Rachel Darnley-Smith.
- Publication by the APMT of a register of research projects into music therapy in the UK.

1992

- European Music Therapy Conference held at Kings College, Cambridge, organised jointly by the APMT and the BSMT. The Chair of the organising committee was music therapist Margaret Heal, and the administrator was Denize Christophers of the BSMT. Three hundred music therapists attended from 23 countries worldwide.

1993

- Publication of *Music Therapy in Health and Education*, edited by Margaret Heal and Tony Wigram.

  This comprised papers from the Cambridge conference and was the first book about music therapy in the UK to be published for over a decade. It heralded a plethora of new publications, supported by publishers Routledge and Jessica Kingsley, who expressed much interest in the growing confidence of music therapists to write about their work.

1994

- Anglia Polytechnic University, Cambridge. First MA (Masters) course in music therapy established by Helen Odell-Miller and Amelia Oldfield.
- Atsain, Music Therapy Trust for Wales was established, with the aim of promoting the development of music therapy in Wales. Phil Tomkins was the Trust's first honorary secretary.

1995

- APMT Supervision scheme launched.

  Newly-qualified music therapists were now required to undergo 32 hours of supervision with an approved supervisor in order to qualify for full membership of the APMT. A complementary scheme was also set up whereby after five years of clinical practice music therapists could apply to a special panel to become approved supervisors. (The name was subsequently changed to 'registered supervisors', 2001.) Pauline Etkin, Director of Nordoff–Robbins Music Therapy Centre, and Ann Sloboda, former Chair of the APMT, took much responsibility for the scheme's development.
- Conference 'Professions in Partnership' held at St Bartholomew's Hospital, London. Chaired by Helen Tyler (Patey), Chair of the BSMT.

  This was a joint venture between the APMT and the BSMT that highlighted the collaboration of music therapists with other professionals, including teachers, speech and language therapists, psychotherapists and psychiatrists.
- National Appeal for Music Therapy.

  The appeal was sponsored jointly by the BSMT and the Music Therapy Charity and raised money for clinical work and research.
- Nordoff–Robbins in Scotland Music Therapy Unit opened.

1996

- State Registration of music therapy was formally ratified in Parliament. Music therapists were received at a special reception to mark the occasion in the House of Commons, Westminster, London.

1997

- Welsh College of Music and Drama, Cardiff. Postgraduate diploma in music therapy set up by music therapists in Wales and Bristol. The course director was Alison Levinge. This was the first British training course to be set up outside England.

1998

- NHS Wales Committee for art, drama and music therapists formed, which through the All-Wales Committee for Healthcare Professions had a direct link to the Welsh Office, and from 1999 to the Welsh Assembly.
- Limerick. First music therapy course in Republic of Ireland began at the World Music Centre. Wendy Magee was the course director.

1999

- APMT formally ratifies a system for Continuing Professional Development.

2000

- 'Celebrating Music Therapy – Our Past, Our Present and Our Future'. Joint APMT/BSMT Millenium Conference at St. Bartholomew's Hospital, London. Guest speakers included representatives of the early days of the profession, Dr Clive Robbins, Professor Leslie Bunt, Angela Fenwick and Rachel Verney.
- First presentation by a music therapist at the Welsh Assembly. Felicity North, arts therapies representative, participated in a presentation by the All-Wales Healthcare Professions Committee to the Health and Social Services Committee.

2002

- Death of Sybil Beresford-Peirse, founder of the Nordoff–Robbins Music Therapy Centre and first head of training.
- Moray House, University of Edinburgh. Music therapy training course in Scotland begins. James Robertson appointed as course director.

- World Congress of Music Therapy Conference held in Oxford, attended by over 900 delegates. Conference planned by the World Federation of Music Therapy, APMT and the BSMT. Conference Director was BSMT and APMT Chair Nigel Hartley.

This calendar of events which spans more than 40 years suggests some clear phases in the life of professional music therapy. The early years (1958–76) involved setting up the profession out of the work of lone individuals, through the development of organisations and the inception of training courses which helped to define music therapy in the UK. In the next phase (1976–90) the profession was required to satisfy the terms of statutory bodies such as the Department of Health and the academic institutions who validated the training courses and awarded research degrees. Recognition of the APMT as the representative body of music therapy was essential to these areas of development. The third phase (1990 to the publication of this book) has seen music therapists becoming actively involved at a statutory level by joining together with the other arts therapy professions to create a seat at the Health Professions Council, the state regulatory body. It has also been a phase of consolidation of the work of those involved in the early years of the profession. From 1992 this has been demonstrated by the writing of many new books and journal articles, together with the creation of websites, and the regular participation of music therapists at national and international conferences.

We began this chapter with a vignette of a music therapy group in a hospital. In the next chapter we will look more deeply at different ways in which some of the pioneers of music therapy developed their work, providing a context for the clinical material described throughout this book.

2

TWO APPROACHES TO
MUSIC THERAPY

At the World Congress of Music Therapy in Washington DC,
USA, in 1999, the international community (Aigen, 1999: 14)
examined five significant models of music therapy: Behavioural
Music Therapy, (Madsen and Madsen, 1968; Madsen, Cotter and
Madsen, 1968) Benenzon Music Therapy (Benenzon, 1981) and the
Bonny Method of Guided Imagery and Music (Goldberg, 1995). The
remaining two, Analytic Music Therapy and Nordoff–Robbins
Music Therapy, originated in Britain, and both have been particularly influential and significant in the development of music therapy
clinical practice, teaching and research, not only in the UK but
worldwide.

Analytic Music Therapy: A Psychotherapeutic Approach

The work of the British music therapist Mary Priestley, which began
at St. Bernard's Hospital in Middlesex, is documented in her book
Music Therapy in Action (1975). She describes how, with her colleagues Gillian Lovett, Peter Wright and Marjorie Wardle, she
developed a variety of music therapy techniques for working with
adults who had emotional, psychological or mental health problems.
St. Bernard's was a sizeable psychiatric hospital, originally built in
the 1830s when it was known as the Hanwell Lunatic Asylum. The
hospital had a tradition of pioneers in the field of psychiatric care,
including the nineteenth-century doctors William Ellis and John
Conolly. Both men advocated new forms of therapeutic treatment,
and Conolly is credited with abolishing all forms of physical
restraint (Weinreb and Hibbert, 1983: 696). Over one hundred years

later, during the 1970s and 1980s, the music therapists were also ready to pioneer new treatments. Their hospital work was broad in its scope, including music and movement sessions and musical performances, in addition to providing group and individual music therapy for patients with serious mental illness or emotional problems. There was also a weekly music club, open to all on a voluntary basis. Patients heard about the sessions by word of mouth and came to find out what was happening, rather than by formal referral. The music club sessions contained a mixture of spontaneous performances of singing and playing from therapists and patients, as well as improvisation. The music club was, 'for those to whom the hospital is home', wrote Priestley (1975: 95), the 'nearest thing to a musical evening in a friend's house that they will experience.'

At the same time, this pioneering music therapy team were developing the method known as Analytic Music Therapy. Initial ideas for a psychodynamic form of music therapy developed out of Priestley's experience of her own psychoanalysis whilst she was undergoing her music therapy training (Priestley, 1995: 129). Although Juliette Alvin's work showed an orientation towards psychoanalytic theory (Bruscia, 1987: 83), professional music therapy training in 1968 had only just begun, and 'music was being used in therapy in a relatively simple and straightforward way'. Priestley writes:

> As I was in analysis with Dr Wooster at that time, [of music therapy training] I was being made aware of subtler, more problematic, and often more conflicting workings of the psyche, with conscious and unconscious moving in different directions sapping the vital energy and causing confusion in the thinking and subsequent behaviour. (1995: 129)

Priestley was also influenced by Alfred Nieman, a composer, who taught free improvisation to music therapy students at the Guildhall School of Music (Darnley-Smith, forthcoming; Hadley, 2001: 122). Nieman believed that free musical expression allowed direct contact with the inner world. Priestley quotes him as saying:

> Music faces us with the realisation that there are two worlds: the inner and the outer. The inner is often incommunicable, a spiritual world which is difficult to enter from the outer world where we normally speak to one another. Music is a bridge for us by which we can reach this inner world. That is why this free expression is so vital for music therapy. (1975: 31)

She began to use insights gained from her analysis in understanding the work with her music therapy patients and subsequently began to consider the music to be an expression of emotion in sound and a link to the unconscious. Priestley's definition of her method was 'the use of words and symbolic music improvisations by the client and therapist for the purpose of exploring the client's inner life and providing the proclivity for growth' (Bruscia, 1987: 115).

Analytic Music Therapy was developed in close collaboration with Wardle and Wright, who also entered personal analysis. Furthermore, the three colleagues decided to meet each week for two hours to:

> ... undertake music therapy experiments on each other before using these techniques on the patients. This was the only way of realising how extraordinarily powerful this therapy could be and thus established the kind of parameters that needed to be laid down in order to provide a reasonably informed background to the work. (Priestley, 1995: 129)

They later named this innovatory means of peer self-learning and psychological support for their work 'Intertherap'. Priestley recommended that Intertherap sessions should take place weekly, as soon after the therapist's own individual analytic psychotherapy as possible. Intertherap sessions would involve each participant taking it in turn to 'be the client'. When they took the role of client, they would openly share their 'inner life', for example, responses to dreams or concerns about family life at home. They used the musical instruments to express their current thoughts. Priestley writes that, following the emotional turmoil of individual psychotherapy, these sessions left them 'physically relaxed' and with 'a feeling of having created a viable sound structured response to life, even though the matters worked through may have been extremely disturbing' (1975: 36). The principle of peers working together in this way is not unique to music therapy. Intertherap has much in common with co-counselling, which also evolved during the 1960s–70s. This was developed by those seeking to 'look afresh at the whole question of authority in the counselling relationship. There is no mystification because they have both learned the same techniques, often from the same person at the same time.' Counsellors train to work together as equals in a 1:1 relationship, where each spend half their time as client and half as therapist, and no money changes hands (Rowan, 1991: 141–2).

Intertherap also developed as a way of training students and other music therapists experientially in Analytic Music Therapy. From the Intertherap experiments, Priestley developed techniques which could address patients' feelings, encouraging them to talk as well as to play. This combination of playing music and talking could lead the patient to a deeper understanding of the underlying psychological conflicts which may have contributed to the illness. Priestley described the purpose of Analytic Music Therapy as 'a way of exploring the unconscious with an analytical music therapist by means of sound expression. It is a way of getting to know oneself, possibly as a greater self than one had realised existed' (1975: 32). Priestley continues:

> A psychiatric patient, for example, may be using her creativity in life to act out the frustration caused by her intruding mother through refusing food, taking overdoses, maintaining self-destructive and denigrating relationships. All this takes vital creative energy. When the music therapist can persuade her to act out some of these communications in sound, immediately the creativity becomes a positive use of energy. (1975: 34)

As already indicated, Analytic Music Therapy sessions typically involve both words and music. The therapist and client discuss the client's concerns. The therapist might then invite the client to suggest a title for an improvisation or the therapist might suggest a title which connects with relevant issues.

The following case example shows the music therapist using the technique of a titled improvisation to help the client to focus on how he feels.

Simon is a young man who has recently disclosed, to the music therapist and other professionals involved in his care, his memories of childhood sexual abuse perpetrated by his uncle. Following a long period in a psychiatric unit, he currently lives in a hostel where he is isolated and lonely. He attends music therapy as an outpatient. At the start of one session, soon after his discharge from the hospital, he focuses again upon memories of childhood, his loneliness, and on the behaviour of the hostel manager who, he feels, has taken a dislike to him. 'The conditions in the hostel are poor,' he says, 'and no one seems to care if the toilets are blocked or the kitchen is never cleaned. The staff just seem too young to cope with everyone, and never have time to talk, beyond trying to arrange what they call community meetings! What a joke!'

The music therapist is worried to hear that a local hostel should apparently be so poorly managed, and feels tempted to voice her concerns in response. Instead, she chooses what she senses might be the relevant therapeutic path for this session.

She decides to focus upon Simon's relationship to his current situation and how this might connect to other experiences in his life. She suggests a title which spontaneously comes into her mind: 'Why don't we play a piece called "Where I find myself living"? Simon agrees, walks directly over to the electric piano and plays with both hands for about ten minutes. He plays long melodic lines in the high treble range of the piano, and holds other notes for a long time in the bass. The therapist plays with him, on the cello, but she finds it almost impossible to engage with Simon's music. She has the feeling that he is completely lost in his music-making and needs to shut her out. She moves to a drum and gently plays single sounds at different intervals, intending him to hear that she is listening to him and that he is not alone. When the music finishes, Simon again starts to talk angrily, this time about the other residents in his hostel. The therapist asks what Simon felt about the music they have just played. Simon answers that his music is 'his black hole'. The therapist asks what he thought about her music and the experience of playing together, but Simon replies that he hardly heard her at all.

In further discussion, Simon was able to see that his music, and his verbal response to it, reflected painful childhood feelings which were being reawakened by the loneliness and neglect he was experiencing in the hostel. The therapist felt that her own experience of Simon's music reflected his ongoing difficulty in being able to trust other people.

Bruscia writes,

A characteristic feature of analytical music therapy is that the client's improvising is often stimulated and guided by feelings, ideas, images, fantasies, memories, events, situations, etc., which the client or therapist has identified as an issue needing therapeutic investigation. These 'titled' improvisations are programmatic or 'referential' in nature in that the music symbolizes or refers to something outside of itself. (1987: 116)

By suggesting a title for the improvisation, the therapist had enabled Simon to link his music directly to his situation. With the help of words, he was able to hear it as symbolising or referring to a part of himself.

The publication of *Music Therapy in Action*, the development of Analytic Music Therapy, and the technique of Intertherap were all influential in the development of music therapy over the ensuing

25 years. Analytic Music Therapy was the first music therapy approach in Britain to name and consider the role of psychotherapeutic concepts such as transference and countertransference (Scheiby, 1998: 214). Other music therapists interested in psychodynamic ideas (Streeter, 1999: 12) began to evolve an approach to music therapy that they called 'psychoanalytically informed music therapy' (Heal, 1989, 1994; John, 1992, 1995).

Although Analytic Music Therapy and Intertherap were not developed into a specific training course in the UK, their ideas have influenced how music therapists are trained, as courses have gradually incorporated the teaching of psychotherapeutic ideas into their syllabuses. Today all courses include some experiential components, such as personal therapy, weekly music therapy groups or groups facilitated by a psychotherapist. The rationale for experiential components in music therapy training was based on the premise that 'One cannot truly learn about psychodynamics [or inter-relating] without learning about oneself, and one rarely learns profound things about oneself without consequent change and growth' (Swiller, Lang and Halperin, 1993: 542–3). For the students of the early 1980s onwards, engaging in a therapeutic process themselves could allow direct knowledge of their own inner world. This reflected the original purpose of Priestley, Wardle and Wright's Intertherap sessions. Priestley writes 'I have made it a personal rule not to use therapeutic techniques on the patients that I have not tried out on myself with colleagues first. When I occasionally break this rule through impatient enthusiasm, I always regret it' (1995: 129).

Priestley's method of Analytic Music Therapy has continued to be used in the UK, Europe, Scandinavia (Scheiby and Nygaard Pederson, 1999: 59) and the US (Scheiby, 1998; Bruscia, 1998). A case example of the technique can be found in Sloboda (1994) in her work with adult clients who have eating disorders. Sloboda describes how the client and therapist improvise music together, which is recorded on tape. After the music has finished, client and therapist listen to the recording and talk about their responses to it. The music therapist encourages the client to comment upon what she experienced in playing the music, what she hears in terms of interaction between the two of them, and to share any thoughts or images which occur. Sloboda found that this way of working, which closely resembles Mary Priestley's model of Analytic Music Therapy, proved helpful in working with clients who were diagnosed with anorexia or bulimia. Sloboda recounts her work with Joanna:

As the sessions progressed this music came to represent a previously despised and repressed part of herself, that needed nurturing. In her own words, two contrasting images or metaphors emerged (images that could be represented visually or in sound). The first, her anorexia, was described as dry, tense, lifeless, rigid, brittle, restless, and rejecting all contact. Joanna improvised on percussion depicting her 'anorexic self' as a 'lifeless skeleton, with rattling bones'.

In this piece she avoided all the resonant instruments, making dull or scratchy sounds, and switched rapidly from one instrument to another.

The other image was associated with emotion, and was always represented by violin and piano improvisations. Joanna described this music as 'fluid, flowing, alive, emotional, resonant, full'.

We discussed the characteristics of these two musical metaphors: the lifeless skeleton, and the life-giving flow. It was possible to reflect on the paradox that, while Joanna greatly preferred the latter, all her self-esteem, identity and confidence had become attached to the former. Joanna identified the deep, resonant qualities of her violin music with the emotional, vulnerable parts of herself that she had 'put on ice'. It was as if she had found a new voice, that she needed to explore and get to know. The violin music served to articulate emotions which Joanna had not yet found words to express. (1994: 257–8)

Sloboda quotes Nolan's view that the potential of music to 'elicit extra-musical associations' is 'its most important contribution to work with this client group. Through these associations the emotions expressed in spontaneous improvisations could be brought to greater consciousness' (1994: 249).

It is as though the music created during sessions provides a mirror for the client, in which they can see a reflection of themselves. The client's self-understanding can develop in a new and different way through music and through the subsequent verbal discussion.

Nordoff–Robbins Music Therapy: A Music-Centred Approach

We began this chapter by stating that Nordoff-Robbins Music Therapy, like Analytic Music Therapy, has been recognised as one of the five international models of music therapy practice. Its founders, however, were apparently unhappy at 'Nordoff–Robbins' being labelled as a model or a method. Robbins warned his students in 1974 that 'all the techniques we give you must be modified, adapted, even ignored, depending upon the children you work with. Otherwise music therapy becomes a prescription and a dogma and an uncreative activity' (Aigen, 1996: 32). Nevertheless, the case studies, research, writings and teachings of the two men have since formed the basis of six training courses, in London (City University), Germany (University of Witten-Herdecke), the US (New York University), South Africa (University of Pretoria), Australia (University of Western Sydney) and Scotland (University of Edinburgh). Although the cultural contexts and academic requirements differ between the various settings, the core philosophy and basic teaching of the approach are clearly identifiable as having their roots in the work of the two pioneers.

Nordoff and Robbins began their collaboration in 1959, when they met by chance in a school where Robbins (b. 1925) was a teacher of children with special needs. Nordoff (1909–77), an American composer and pianist, was visiting the school to give a piano recital to the staff. The school, at Sunfield Children's Home in Worcestershire, England, was run on the educational principles laid down by the anthroposophical philosopher Rudolf Steiner, which stressed the importance and relevance to children's development of music and the arts. Nordoff was then invited by Dr Herbert Geuter, the school's psychologist, to contribute to a project in which he was studying the application of the arts in therapy. Nordoff was to use his skills as a pianist and composer to engage the children in improvised music-making so that their responses could be assessed. Robbins, who had a particular interest in using music with his pupils, became Nordoff's partner in the ensuing research project. (Nordoff and Robbins, 1992).

In their time together at Sunfield School between 1959 and 1960, Nordoff and Robbins worked with both individuals and groups of children with a wide range of needs, disabilities and impairments. Initially, each child was brought to the music room and was given simple percussion instruments to explore, such as a drum, cymbal, tambourine or chimes. While Robbins facilitated or encouraged the child's participation, Nordoff improvised at the piano and with his voice, reflecting and responding to whatever sounds and reactions the child gave. As Nordoff said later in an interview for BBC television:

> We meet the tempo of whatever the child is doing, the tempo of his walking, his head-banging, his pacing up and down, his rocking. We take the sounds he might make, whether it is screaming, or screaming-crying, and we give this back to him in music, so that he has a new experience of what he does habitually. And then, gradually, the goals we have to work for emerge as the child shows us 'Here I am, this is me, I can only do this.' (BBC, 1976)

This ability of all children to create sound and rhythm and to respond to it in others (which we have already seen described by Trevarthen and Malloch in Chapter 1 as 'communicative musicality'), in Nordoff and Robbins' writings was defined as the concept of the Music Child.

> The Music Child is ... the individualized musicality inborn in each child: the term has reference to the universality of musical sensitivity – the heritage of complex sensitivity to the ordering and relationship of tonal and rhythmic movement; it also points to the distinctly personal significance of each child's musical responsiveness. (1977: 1)

This responsiveness, however, was not immediately forthcoming with all of Nordoff and Robbins' young clients. Because of their physical, emotional or psychological difficulties many were remote, scarcely aware of themselves and others, or confused and chaotic. This was where the musician-therapist's skill in building a relationship through music or 'meeting the music child' (1977: 1) was crucial.

Of these early experiments in Sunfield School, Nordoff and Robbins wrote:

> These explorations disclosed that each child reacted differently to music. Many expressed their individuality or state of development in their relationship to a specific element of music. One child would be engaged in assimilating the element of structure, another lived in the melodic element, while yet another found security in the basic beat ... The style and mood of the music that was played evoked important responses from them. Empirical work led to the improvising of Oriental music, medieval church music, eastern European music, and other styles with different geographical and historical origins. The most romantic music was needed by one boy, while yet another required the most dissonant. (1985: 34)

Even at this early stage of their work together, it is clear how much importance they placed on finding the music which each child 'needed'. Paul Nordoff used his own instrument, the piano, which he saw as the medium most able to provide a wide range of rhythm, melody, harmony and timbre, to create a rich variety of musical and emotional experiences. After leaving Sunfield, the pair visited many Steiner schools and hospitals to demonstrate their newly-evolving ideas and found that they encountered some criticism from colleagues:

> ... we were seriously challenged to justify our use of music. Many workers found much of it too loud, too dissonant and too rhythmic. They were of the opinion that music for handicapped children should be soothing, rather soft, conventionally harmonious, and, if active, not stimulating ... But

this was more a mild form of entertainment than a music therapy, and could become a subduing, conditioning factor in a child's life. Music, we fervently believed, could be more than this. (1985: 44–5)

This fervent belief in the power of the music to reach into the emotional life of a child was the cornerstone of the Nordoff–Robbins philosophy.

After the period at Sunfield School, Paul Nordoff gave up his performing career, and spent the rest of his life as a music therapist, researcher and teacher. He returned to the US with Robbins where their work attracted research funding from the National Institute of Mental Health. They became part of a team in a day-care unit for autistic children under the auspices of the University of Pennsylvania in Philadelphia. Here they were able to extend their early diagnostic work and to begin detailed research into the effectiveness of improvised music in bringing about change, both in the musical relationship and in the daily lives of the children. Central to this period of Nordoff and Robbins' work was the development of methods of analysis and evaluation, which were required when working in a multi-disciplinary research team headed by psychologists. They devised three rating scales, two of which have been published and since used regularly by music therapists (1977: 177–208). The names of the rating scales, *Scale 1: Child-Therapists Relationship in Musical Activity* and *Scale 2: Musical Communicativeness*, indicate the musical orientation of the scales. A particular feature of Scale 1 is that it assesses the relationship in terms of both Participation and Resistiveness. As they wrote:

Not all response in therapy was participatory: with autistic, post-autistic, or other emotionally disturbed children, resistiveness appeared in many forms to impede or *influence* the development of relationship. With many, resistiveness was a corollary to participation – a progressive response was immediately preceded and/or followed by one that was resistive in some way. (1977: 181)

The scales were used in conjunction with a tape recording of each session, which would be analysed, indexed (using tape counter numbers to mark significant moments) and then assessed. It is important to note that the scales were not designed to give a score or to measure a client's ability. Rather, they were intended to help therapists and, in particular, students, to develop:

- acute listening and careful clinical observation;
- objectivity and a sense of perspective;
- a sense of clinical direction;

- a professional language in which to describe the work; and
- communication with other professionals.

During the period in Pennsylvania, 1962–67, Nordoff and Robbins gathered much clinical material on tape and wrote it up in the form of case studies. They also published several volumes of 'Playsongs' which had their origins in spontaneously improvised songs from individual and group therapy sessions.

Nordoff and Robbins returned to Britain from the US in 1974 at the invitation of a British music therapist, Sybil Beresford-Peirse, to teach the first Nordoff–Robbins training course, based on their approach to improvisational music therapy. The training, which took place in a children's hospital, was specifically designed to train musicians who had a high level of piano skills to become therapists, working with children with special needs. An active fundraising committee purchased premises in 1980, which became the first Nordoff–Robbins Music Therapy Centre, housing the training course, a clinic and research facilities, with Sybil Beresford-Peirse as director and head of training. After Paul Nordoff's death, Clive Robbins continued to teach, research and write about their combined work and, with his wife Carol Robbins, was responsible for setting up the Nordoff–Robbins Music Therapy Center and Training Course in New York.

Since 1974, Nordoff–Robbins-based courses have expanded to include a wider client range, including babies, non-impaired clients, and older adults, and the use of other instruments in addition to the piano. The teaching has also broadened to reflect more recent ideas prevalent in music therapy practice, including influences from psychodynamic thinking, musicology, aesthetics and infant psychology. The music-centred premise, however, on which the work began at Sunfield School remains of central significance.

3

MUSIC AND THE THERAPEUTIC PROCESS

Sally was a nurse who had just begun working in a residential unit, situated in the grounds of a London hospital, for adults with long-term mental health problems. She was helping Rachel, the music therapist, prepare for a weekly music therapy group to which five of the residents belonged. As they were setting out the instruments and Rachel was explaining to Sally how she could contribute to the session, another nurse, Monica, ran into the room. Laughing, she picked up a tambourine and started to beat a fast rhythmic pattern, dancing and crying 'Hey, Hey!' in time to her playing. Sally and Rachel laughed too. Sally then asked 'What is music therapy? What does it do?'

Rachel replied by asking if she could describe Monica's playing.

*'It's **very** energetic!' said Sally.*

'What might that tell you about her as a person?'

Sally thought for a moment and then said, 'Well, that's how Monica is sometimes – all fast and energetic, like the tambourine.'

Rachel then asked the nurses if they had noticed that the atmosphere in the room had changed as Monica struck the tambourine, and that they had all become more relaxed. Both nurses agreed and laughed again, a little self-consciously, before realising that it was now time to focus their thoughts on the residents who were about to enter the room.

What better place to begin than with a description of live impromptu music-making, for, within this short musical exchange, some fundamental precepts of music therapy can be observed. Monica, in playing the tambourine, had spontaneously:

- improvised sound, rhythm and movement;
- interacted with those around her; and
- communicated something about herself.

Rachel answered Sally's question 'What is music therapy?' by drawing on their shared experience. When members of the Executive Committee of the Association of Professional Music Therapists came to answer the same question in 1990, they were drawing on the experience of their colleagues over the previous 30 years. They wrote:

> Music Therapy provides a framework in which a mutual relationship is set up between client and therapist. The growing relationship enables change to occur, both in the condition of the client and in the form that the therapy takes. The Music Therapist works with a variety of clients of all ages in group and individual settings. Their problems and handicaps may be emotional, physical, mental or psychological in nature. By using music creatively in a clinical setting, the therapist seeks to establish an interaction, a shared musical experience leading to the pursuit of therapeutic goals. (APMT, 1990)

To arrive at this complex definition, however, the therapists were making certain assumptions about the nature of music, which we will now summarise.

Six Basic Assumptions

1   That music is a universal medium whose elements of rhythm, pitch, timbre and melody are found worldwide.
2   That music can be very broadly defined as being any 'vocal, instrumental or mechanical sounds that have rhythm, melody or harmony' (*New Penguin English Dictionary*, p. 914).
3   That psychological, neurological and physiological responses to music may remain unimpaired by illness or injury.
4   That the use of sound as an expressive medium pre-dates the acquisition of language.
5   That the act of making sounds freely upon musical instruments provides a non-verbal means of communication and self-expression which embodies or expresses a person's whole self.

6   That a wide range of feelings and emotions may be experienced in response to musical sounds, whether pre-composed or improvised.

Let us now take a closer look at these six assumptions.

1   THAT MUSIC IS A UNIVERSAL MEDIUM WHOSE ELEMENTS OF RHYTHM, PITCH, TIMBRE AND MELODY ARE FOUND WORLDWIDE   The psychotherapist and writer Anthony Storr begins his book *Music and the Mind* by stating, 'No culture so far discovered lacks music' (1992: 1). Music therapists work with the assumption that we all have a relationship with music which is part of an expression of who we are. Ansdell describes musical sounds as being an intrinsic part of human beings:

> We make and experience music because we have bodies which have pulses and tones, tensions and resolutions, phrasing of actions, bursts of intensity, repetitions and development. Music gives us in short, access to a whole world of experience: bodily, emotionally, intellectually, and socially. (1995: 8)

We have already seen, in Chapter 1, the extent to which music is used in many societies, both personally and socially, and that musicality is innate, not restricted to a select few. Furthermore, music has the propensity to draw people together into a group. John Sloboda states that, throughout the world, music is made up of simple rhythmic patterns, which provide the means for groups of people to play together at the same time. He continues:

> Without reference points [in music] it would be impossible for people to make the necessary anticipatory and planned adjustments to bring their behaviour into co-ordination with others, and thus make musical behaviour the structured *social* phenomenon that it is the world over. (1985: 259)

2   THAT MUSIC CAN BE VERY BROADLY DEFINED AS BEING ANY 'VOCAL, INSTRUMENTAL OR MECHANICAL SOUNDS THAT HAVE RHYTHM, MELODY OR HARMONY'   In music therapy we accept a broad definition of music, so that sounds produced in a session might include:

- the raw sound of a human voice or an infants' cry;
- the most crafted of sounds forming a musical composition;
- spontaneous sounds freely improvised, without conscious regard for structure or form;
- functional sounds made by or upon objects which are not musical instruments, such as the shutting of a door or the moving of a chair; or

- electronically produced sounds such as those produced by a vibroacoustic bed (see Chapter 1).

This breadth of definition is important because it is sometimes assumed that music therapists only use particular music specially designed for a positive effect. Pavlicevic writes:

> For music therapy, as we know, is not about making (or playing) 'nice' music – and this is difficult for musicians to absorb. As musicians we want phrases that cadence, harmonic structures that emerge from our cultural conventions … we want balance, symmetry, some kind of resolution – even in (so-called) 'free improvisation'. But in clinical improvisation we are uncovered – it is as though music, as we know it, fails us. In music therapy we need to create sounds on the spot, to meet whatever the child, adult or old person is doing; to meet however that person is 'being' in that moment. And this [does] not necessarily 'fit' with musical convention – of whatever culture. (1999: 25)

3   THAT PSYCHOLOGICAL, NEUROLOGICAL AND PHYSIOLOGICAL RESPONSES TO MUSIC MAY REMAIN UNIMPAIRED BY ILLNESS OR INJURY   Music can sometimes make sense to people where other forms of communication, such as words or body language, cannot be understood, for example, where the client is suffering from severe dementia as a result of Alzheimer's disease. Indeed, Aldridge and Brandt write:

> The responsiveness of clients with Alzheimer's disease to music is a remarkable phenomenon. While language deterioration is a feature of cognitive deficit, musical abilities appear to be preserved. This may be because the fundamentals of language are musical and are prior to semantic and lexical functions, in language development. (1991: 29)

Music can be an immediate form of expression where words cannot be found or seem too dangerous, such as when intense anger or rage is being experienced by the client. It is also a resource for clients who have not developed the use of verbal language for organic or psychological reasons. Music therapy works on the assumption that music can be used by anyone, however severely cognitively, physically or emotionally impaired. Usher suggests why this might be. She writes:

> Music so closely correlates with body rhythms, intonation, and the mobility of emotions that it provides a unique interface between sensations provoked in the mind and other neurological events. Music can function to bypass other areas of the brain which may be damaged or make links to underdeveloped areas; it organises many disparate events in a global way. (1998: 4)

4   THAT THE USE OF SOUND AS AN EXPRESSIVE MEDIUM PRE-DATES THE ACQUISITION OF LANGUAGE   We have seen in Chapter 1 that we are born with innate musicality, together with the means to express ourselves through sound, and so to communicate with those around us. The research of Trevarthen and Malloch (2000: 7) shows how, as the earliest parent–infant communications cannot rely upon linguistic meaning, communication takes place through the use of expressive sounds or 'the prosody of the infant-directed speech', together with facial and gestural movements. Music therapists have adapted these intuitively improvised and non-verbal methods of communication into a sophisticated means of musical communication for expressive and therapeutic ends. Pavlicevic has explored the relationship between clinical improvisation and early communication in her theoretical concept of Dynamic Form, which, she suggests, 'clarifies the interface between music and emotional form in MT [music therapy] improvisation.' (2001: 276)

5   THAT THE ACT OF MAKING SOUNDS FREELY UPON MUSICAL INSTRUMENTS PROVIDES A NON-VERBAL MEANS OF COMMUNICATION AND SELF-EXPRESSION WHICH EMBODIES OR EXPRESSES A PERSON'S WHOLE SELF   Music therapists work with the assumption that the music improvised in sessions is an embodiment or expression of the client in any one moment. We saw in the story of Monica and Sally how the music reflected Monica's character and also affected the relationships between the people in the room.

This was also the experience of Nordoff and Robbins in their early work in music therapy with children in Sunfield School (see Chapter 2) when they wrote:

> The children were making musical self-portraits in the way they were reacting to music thus improvised. Each was different, and it was becoming evident that there must be a direct connection between an individual's pathology, his personality, and the musical self-portrait he [or she] revealed; that the reaction to music in each case could be descriptive of the psychological condition. (1992: 34)

6   THAT A WIDE RANGE OF FEELINGS AND EMOTIONS MAY BE EXPERIENCED IN RESPONSE TO MUSICAL SOUNDS, WHETHER PRE-COMPOSED OR IMPROVISED   In music therapy we use music as an encounter with feeling and emotion which forms the basis for the therapeutic relationship. Pavlicevic writes that: 'In music therapy emotional creativity is sounded *through* the musical act; music and emotion are 'fused,' so to speak. The one presents the other'. (1995: 52)

Where clients are verbal, music therapy can involve talking about the music and about feelings. This can enable both client and therapist to articulate their experiences and to think about what any particular moment might mean. Although music cannot itself be translated into words, for many clients this kind of verbal dialogue, alongside a musical dialogue, forms an important part of the therapeutic process. For other clients, however, it is not possible or helpful to analyse the music in words – indeed, sometimes the music simply speaks for itself. Trevarthen and Malloch write of music's expressive potential:

> A human being making any kind of musical sound – improvising, recreating from memory, reading a score, or responding in therapy – is expressing purposes that can communicate. Actually or potentially, making music is an act of intersubjectivity, a form of behaviour that offers direct information on human motives, from which other humans can sense what underlies a person's actions and experiences. (2000: 4)

These six basic assumptions about music are integral to the practice of improvisational music therapy as practised in the UK today. We will now look at what we mean by improvisation within the context of music therapy, and how this is different from improvising or extemporising in other settings.

What is improvisation?

Musical improvisation has been defined by the APMT as: 'Any combination of sounds and silence spontaneously created within a framework of beginning and ending' (1985: 4). Improvisation is integral to all music-making, whether the performer is following strict instructions or whether the music is spontaneously improvised in the moment. Pavlicevic reminds us that improvisation has always been part of musical performance: 'Before music was notated, oral tradition ensured that songs and pieces were kept alive through performance, and each performer added something distinctive to the music, which transformed it, albeit subtly' (1997: 73).

Notation is no barrier to improvisation, though; it is possible to find musicians improvising, even during the performance of the most carefully notated music. Improvisation might happen when a musician finds a new way of phrasing a melody or emphasising a certain rhythm, even after having played the piece many times. The new idea may transform the performance for the listeners, while the other players may respond with new ideas of their own. Another moment when a musician could need to improvise is when he makes a mistake, for example, coming in at the wrong bar, and then has to find a way to weave his part back into the right place. Ansdell describes an example from a jazz improvisation by pianist Keith Jarrett. Here the genre of the music allows the mistake not only to be woven into the music, but to be used as a spontaneous new idea:

> Jarrett has set up a repetitive ostinato pattern in his left hand, but then seems to miss the 'right note' (according to the pattern). However, he has such musical flexibility that he instantly uses the 'mistake' to create something new – starting the next repetition of the figure on the 'wrong' note and 'correcting' it upwards. This does not sound like a mechanical correction but an inspired detail which then changes the course of the music. (1995: 24)

Many contemporary styles of western music, such as jazz and soul, are based around improvisation within a predictable musical framework. Some musicians, for example, The London Musician's Collective, are also interested in free improvisation and perform works that are spontaneous in style, duration and content. Musicians who incorporate improvisation into their playing often relate that they have gained an emotional experience of their fellow musicians through improvising together. To them, improvisation is not just an artistic manipulation of melody, rhythm and harmony – they are improvising in response to their collective experience of hearing each other in the music. This brings us very close to describing what the therapeutic relationship in music therapy can offer.

Clinical Improvisation

Clinical improvisation is a specialised form of musical improvisation, which is used within the framework of music therapy. It is defined by the Association of Professional Music Therapists as 'musical improvisation with a specific therapeutic meaning and purpose in an environment facilitating response and interaction' (APMT, 1985: 5).

Both therapist and client are freely involved in making live music with a variety of musical instruments which are specially chosen by the music therapist so that the client is able to make sounds without needing prior knowledge or skill. These will include tuned and un-tuned percussion instruments, such as xylophones, glockenspiels, drums of all types, cymbals, tambourines, chimes and bells and percussion instruments of different ethnic origins. There may also be pipes and whistles, stringed instruments, either plucked or bowed, and keyboards, including the piano. The music therapist may use their own instrument, be it piano, wind or strings, or may join the client in playing the other instruments available, while in some cases the clients may bring instruments of their own to a session. The aim of clinical improvisation is that the spontaneous sounds or musical elements become the means and focus of communication, expression and reflection between therapist and client. Within a confidential and reliable setting, free from interruptions, conducive to the establishing of a trusting relationship, the client is invited to play freely upon the instruments. The therapist listens and responds, also upon the musical instruments, and so the therapeutic relationship begins. The use of free musical improvisation means that, on the whole, therapists do not prepare what musical material they are going to use. Instead, they wait to see what music emerges between them and their clients when they start to play or sing together: the music is made up there and then.

Starting an Improvisation

The setting was the music therapy room in a day hospital for older adults with mental health problems. It was the first meeting between Susan, an elderly woman who was in the early stages of dementia, and Rachel, the music therapist. She showed Susan the instruments and invited her to wander around the room trying out any that she liked. At first Susan just looked at the instruments, touching some of them and turning them over. Then she sat down in front of a small drum which was standing on the floor. Picking up a stick, she made a soft sound on the drum. Rachel picked up a tambour and played a similar sound in response. Susan looked at the therapist with surprise, before making another sound. Rachel waited briefly and there was a slight tension in the silence. She played once again, in response, keeping to the same volume of sound. Susan quickly played once more, and again Rachel responded, but this time without stopping, a slow regular sound. Susan copied Rachel's sounds, and for a few moments they played together.

In this first meeting the therapist had no plan or expectation of what would be the right or wrong way to play with the client. Anything

Susan played, or the silence that was created when she did not play, provided a basis from which the music therapist, trusting her own instincts, could find ways to form a musical relationship.

Performance Improvisation and Clinical Improvisation: A Distinction

The difference between what we will now call performance improvisation and clinical improvisation is one of purpose and intent rather than the actual sounds that are made. Sometimes the music created in a music therapy session could be mistaken by an uninformed listener for free improvisation in a performance setting. Indeed, in both clinical improvisation and performance improvisation, musical ideas are allowed to emerge creatively and to unfold in the moment as the players create sounds in their own way.

The difference lies in how the purpose of the improvisation affects the *direction* the improvised music might take:

- In **music therapy** the purpose of improvising music is to develop a therapeutic relationship in order to pursue clinical goals.
- In a **performance setting** the purpose of improvising music is to develop musical relationships in order to pursue an artistic goal for its own sake.

Let us look at this difference in a little more detail.

Free Improvisation in a Performance Setting

It is impossible to play live music with others without entering into some kind of relationship. In a performance, however, the purpose of improvisation is to create a piece of music for its own sake, whether in the context of a rehearsal, a recording, or experimentation between musicians. The performing musician, for example, might start to play a melody on the xylophone. The next musician might find a regular rhythm to fit with the melody, possibly to create tension, or a sense of contrast. This is not to suggest that the making of and experimenting with musical sounds within non-clinical settings has no effect upon the relationships between the musicians involved or upon their audience. Nor is the possibility denied that an individual's intention in improvising music in a performance setting might be in order to interact with others in a group. However, musicians improvising for the purpose of music-making will constantly be making musical decisions towards expressive or artistic rather than therapeutic ends. Pavlicevic writes about some research which she and a colleague undertook that involved a live experiment investigating this distinction:

> In a collaborative project with Sandra Brown, [Brown and Pavlicevic, 1996] in which we took turns at improvising together (1) as music therapist and client, and (2) as musicians improvising together, we found in analysing the tapes that when we were playing as therapists, it was not the music that dictated the improvisation, but how we experienced the other person, the client, in the music. As musicians, we found that we could 'play', literally and indulgently, allowing the spontaneously created music to emerge and develop and dictate the improvisation. (1997: 66–7)

Free Improvisation in a Clinical Setting
In a clinical improvisation the therapist finds musical ways of relating to the client by carefully listening to and observing the client's musical responses in relation to their own. The therapist will be assessing:

- How is the client communicating – through instruments, voice, movement or facial expression?
- Who initiates the playing – client or therapist?
- Does the client stop playing when the therapist starts?
- Does the client appear to notice the therapist's response?
- Does the client let the therapist support or accompany?
- Does the client play a musical monologue or allow the therapist space to play too?
- Does the client respond to the sounds of the therapist in what feels like an interactive musical dialogue?

These, and the many other different ways in which the client might respond musically to the therapist, not only provide clues about the client's capacity for relationship, but also indicate the musical direction in which the therapist might proceed. This means that during the improvisation, the music therapist is constantly making musical decisions towards clinical ends. The direction that the improvisation takes is affected by its clinical rather than musical purpose. For example, our client Susan, who had started music therapy by playing a drum, might move on to experiment with sounds on a xylophone. The therapist might add a simple rhythm to support her playing. This rhythm fits in musically, but the purpose of playing in this particular way is not to create an aesthetically pleasing piece of music for its own sake. Rather, the therapist is intuitively seeking to provide an appropriate communication to the patient, in this example connected to the therapist's aim of creating a feeling of safety.

Understanding a distinction between performance improvisation and clinical improvisation is integral to the process of developing as a music therapist. The relationship with the patient, through music, constantly needs to be held at the forefront of the therapist's mind, informing clinical and musical intentions.

Developing a Music Therapy Relationship

So far we have focused upon the musical aspects of music therapy practice, but there are other aspects too which can be considered significant. For example, a child client may:

- become preoccupied with switching the lights on and off;
- hide behind the piano;
- play with a toy rather than the instruments;
- want to leave the session early; or
- use the instruments in non-musical ways.

An adult client may:

- stop playing and begin to talk about a personal issue;
- suddenly leave the room immediately after playing; or
- always arrive late for the session.

To ignore these actions because they do not have an obvious connection to the music would be to miss important communications from the client. Responding to the client's music alone is not enough; a framework of therapy, together with a means of understanding both the musical and extra-musical exchanges is, in our experience, essential. In our approach to music therapy we treat all events in a music therapy session as significant and potentially linked. The two case studies that follow, first of a child and secondly of an adult, illustrate the type of extra-musical considerations which occur in music therapy.

Case Study: Paul

Paul was five years old and attended weekly music therapy sessions with Helen. He had a diagnosis of Angelman's syndrome, which is a genetic condition causing both physical and cognitive disabilities and in particular, an inability to acquire speech. He was a lively and active little boy and was always eager to take part in the sessions, waiting impatiently for Helen to fetch him, with his nose pressed against the glass waiting room door. Once he was in the therapy room, however, he would run to each instrument in turn, play a few beats, then throw the beaters on the floor, and go to the door waving 'bye-bye'. This response in music mirrored the way Paul was at home, flitting from one toy to another and soon losing interest and concentration. After five minutes he felt he had done everything he could and that it was time to go back to his mother. Any attempt to prolong the session beyond this point caused Paul to become anxious and distressed. At first it felt appropriate to end the sessions after just a few minutes, so that Paul could see that his mother was still there, waiting for him. His reaction to the therapy reflected the difficulty he experienced in separating from his mother, particularly at bedtime when it was very hard for him to settle down on his own. In the early sessions Helen improvised short, predictable musical structures in the form of musical games to motivate Paul to continue beyond his natural attention span. The music was playful, in the style and character of nursery rhymes. Gradually the sessions expanded in length, and Paul was able to manage to stay for a full half-hour session.

Later in Paul's therapy, separation anxiety became a renewed and problematic feature of his life. A regular weekend away from home in respite care had been offered to Paul, and because of his chronic sleeplessness, this was a potential lifeline for his weary parents. Paul, however, found this very distressing and began to stay awake all night, which in turn was upsetting for the family. Each week he began to cry as soon as the door of the music therapy room closed, calling for Mummy. Although it was hard for Helen to hear him crying, it was important now that she did not end the session early. Helen knew that her task was not to try to comfort Paul, to cuddle him, or distract him from his crying, but, rather, to reflect his sense of sadness and loss in the music. She could not make everything alright for Paul, but she could help him to accept and tolerate the pain of parting. In one session, as she played a poignant melody in a minor key, singing, 'Paul is here, Helen is here, Mummy is there, waiting for Paul', Paul lay down on the floor and rested his cheek on a small drum as though it were a pillow. He sighed deeply, vocalizing 'ma-ma' in the tonality of the *music. At this point, the cheerful nursery tunes had gone and playing the instruments was of secondary importance to meeting the expression of Paul's feelings. It was as though the half-hour sessions, with their consistency and regularity, had become a weekly rehearsal for Paul in parting from his mother. Helen and Paul were both able to get through this difficult time and to explore, in the music, the deep feelings of loss and anxiety which it seemed Paul always carried with him. After a few months of patient work, the situation improved and Paul began to accept his respite weekends as part of his life. Hard though it had been, keeping the time structure of the sessions, despite Paul's distress, was vital to the process.*

In the second case example, the therapist is listening to changes in the client's music, but is also attending to her own responses, both musical and emotional.

Case Study: Felipe

Felipe was a man in his early thirties who, following an assessment session, attended individual music therapy for short-term work over 12 sessions. As a child he suffered from neglect. Since his teenage years he had many relationships, mostly with men, some much older than himself. He had established a painting and decorating business during his twenties, but after two years it began to fail and he was eventually left unemployed. Since the collapse of his business he had become very isolated and depressed and was referred by his GP to a mental health day hospital. The reason for his referral was so that he could receive support, and to engage in therapy which might facilitate some self-understanding regarding his depression and general life situation. He asked if he could go to music therapy, as he told his key worker, an occupational therapist, that he wanted to try 'all the arts therapies'. During the first two sessions, he chose to play the xylophone, from time to time adding extra instruments such as a small drum, shaker, and temple blocks. Rachel, the music therapist, for the most part played the piano, although at times she moved to a conga drum or another xylophone. Rachel found that the music flowed easily between them and that she could comfortably either accompany Felipe's playing or introduce new melodic or harmonic ideas. In turn he was inventive in his musical ideas, finding new sounds in the instruments he tried. However, during the third session Felipe began to play more heavily and monotonously, and Rachel found herself beginning to struggle; the pace had slowed down, and finding a way to respond had suddenly become harder. From now on, the sessions seemed an interminable length, and Rachel found herself wanting to fall asleep or end the session early. Her musical ideas had ceased to flow and she could no longer play in response to Felipe. It felt difficult to be in the room with him and her mind started wandering away from the therapy to everyday matters in her own life. Over the next few weeks she tried various ways to engage Felipe, including listening to him talking about his search for employment and a new place to live. He would also talk about the difficult relationships he had with his parents, who were separated, and in particular with his father, upon whom he was dependent for money. Rachel occasionally made supportive comments and, as she learnt more about his life, tried to understand with him what was causing his depression. She also tried to keep the musical focus alive in sessions, suggesting different instruments they both might play, and specific musical idioms such as 'the blues' that they might use as a structure for their improvisations. But nothing seemed to make any difference to the lifeless music and the sleepy atmosphere which prevailed in the room.

After the initial two sessions, it became very hard for Rachel to communicate with Felipe and it seemed as if he had stopped wanting to speak to her through his music-making. One could speculate that this was also a pattern in Felipe's life, of getting close to people quickly but being unable to develop the relationship, and cutting himself off. At this point, when it felt that an impasse had been reached, it was very important that Rachel did not abandon the therapy, feeling that it was not going anywhere, but that she should remain in the uncomfortable position of sharing Felipe's difficult feelings. Why did she consider this so important and how could it be achieved? We shall now use Felipe's story to describe the purpose of having a framework in music therapy.

Framework of Therapy: Preparing the Ground

The concept of a therapeutic frame or framework, which is essential to good practice in all kinds of therapy, has been described in detail by Gray (1994). She cites the work of the art therapist Marion Milner (1952) who was 'the first to apply this concept using the metaphor of an artist's frame' (Gray 1994: 5). In the same way that a picture frame creates a boundary round the art work and contains it, so the therapeutic framework contains the work of the therapist and client. Although, ideally, the frame is maintained and protected, Gray stresses that much can be learned from the breaks or mistakes which inevitably occur in the course of therapy. We shall see some examples of this in the following section.

1 Regularity of Sessions

The therapeutic framework calls for regular sessions, as well as consistency of time and place. This regularity establishes a vital rhythm to the work, which further contributes to the client experiencing the therapy setting as being safe. Regularity also relates to the contract or agreement set up with the client. In some settings, for example, an acute psychiatric ward, this might be simply a verbal agreement between the music therapist and client to attend a single session later that day. In other venues, a contract might be established, written or verbal, where a client attends for a period of months or years. With some clients where their agreement to begin music therapy cannot be given, for example, where a child is very young or has severe learning disabilities, a contract might be set up with a parent or carer. However, the music therapist can then spend a period of assessment trying to establish whether or not this client is responsive to music therapy, or apparently wishes to proceed. Overall, it is crucial to have a basic contract whereby therapist and client, or a representative of the client, agree:

- the time for meeting;
- the nature of the sessions, i.e. a single session, a session or series of sessions for assessment, or a series of sessions for ongoing treatment;
- the frequency of sessions (once weekly, more than once weekly); and
- a fee (for therapists in private practice).

This contract establishes that both parties are going to work together, the therapist offering professional skills and the client actively seeking help, forming the essential basis for establishing what is known as a working alliance. In the case of Felipe, the agreed contract was short-term, for 12 weeks only, at the specific request of the day hospital multi-disciplinary team who wanted to avoid clients becoming too dependent on therapy. It is possible to speculate in retrospect that this arrangement felt unsafe to Felipe, and that, by the third week, the end of the sessions seemed all too imminent. It was disappointing and frustrating for the music therapist, but no surprise, that he did not attend his last two sessions. It also demonstrated the extent of his emotional fragility, which had not been apparent in the initial assessment. In terms of the therapist learning about the client, the sessions Felipe missed were as revealing as those he attended.

2 Time Boundaries

As we saw earlier in this chapter in the case study of Paul, a clear time structure is very important in order to create a sense of psychological safety. Felipe's music therapy sessions took place at the same time each week and always lasted for one hour. This allowed the changes in the content of the sessions to be seen very clearly. The passing of a set amount of time creates a structure within which the free improvisations or other events in a session can take place. If the therapist, Rachel, had decided to end each session whenever it seemed that they had 'run out of music,' she would not have experienced the part of Felipe that found it difficult to play and to sustain a relationship. Felipe was always on time for his session and Rachel would find him waiting on a chair near the music therapy room. Rachel experienced his punctuality as bringing some energy and communicating his commitment to the session. If she had sometimes started a few minutes late, the energy gained by his timekeeping would have been lost; Felipe might have felt that it made no difference to the therapist whether he was on time or late, or even whether he had come at all.

3 Privacy of the Music Therapy Room

This room, which was sometimes used for other purposes within the day hospital, was specially booked for the music therapy sessions. This was not only a practical consideration, but also ensured that a reliable space was created, free from interruptions. When a client such as Felipe engages in music therapy, he is allowing his vulnerability to be shared with the therapist. If a session is held in a room which is liable to interruption, it is impossible to build up a sense of trust and safety. Furthermore, therapeutic work of this kind takes an enormous amount of concentration, on the part of both therapist and client, which can be irreparably broken by an interruption. If this happens, the therapist invariably spends the remainder of the session feeling guilty at having failed to protect the therapy space from intrusion, or angry about the lack of respect for the therapy shown by colleagues. Such feelings provide further distraction from the central task of the session.

It is important to mention that the establishing and maintenance of a safe setting is not a simple task. Precise time-keeping requires much commitment from the therapist, particularly when it may be regarded as unnecessary within organisations where meetings frequently begin a few minutes late and patients are not surprised to be kept waiting beyond their appointment times.

Neither is it always realistic or appropriate to insist on keeping to rigid time boundaries. There are occasions when other needs may have to take precedence. For example, the music therapist arrives on an acute psychiatric ward to find the way blocked by nurses who are attempting to calm a violent client. The session has to wait. A ward for elderly people might be in quarantine due to an infection, making it impossible for a group session to take place. In a school, where the music therapist may work for only one or two days each week, considerable persistence and patience may be needed to establish regularity of sessions. Special activities or the needs of the curriculum may take precedence over pre-arranged therapy times, and the therapist may arrive at the school to find that the children have gone on an outing or are involved in a special project.

These breaks in the frame can be very discouraging for the therapist who may feel overworked or ill. In all these scenarios it is important that the music therapist does not abandon the therapeutic frame, but keeps it in mind to think about the possible unconscious reasons for the interruption or simply to acknowledge that the interruption has taken place.

4   Endings

It has been said that the moments of taking off and landing are potentially the most hazardous for the pilot and passengers of an aeroplane. Beginnings and endings are most certainly times of great importance and sensitivity in music therapy. The whole course of therapy can be greatly affected by attending to the points raised in sections 1–3 above, at the outset of the therapy. Louis Zinkin, writing about analytic psychotherapy, stated that 'there is a great difference between bringing something to an end and just stopping' (1994: 18). Embedded in the process of therapy, as in life, is the fact that it will end. The end of treatment is not necessarily the moment at which the desired outcome is reached but, like the beginning and the middle, is an essential stage.

Sometimes for various reasons, such as the unexpected transfer of a client to another school or hospital, the therapy does just stop. Here the therapist may be able to find ways of ending the therapy, for example, by making contact with the client through a visit or letter. Particularly where the client had no control over such arrangements, this might be considered essential. In other circumstances, such as the death of the client, the ending might have been long anticipated and the process of saying goodbye incorporated. If the death is sudden, the therapist might end the work for themselves through reflection in supervision. Attending a client's funeral may also be an important part of the ending, whether or not the therapist contributes music to the occasion. In contrast, planned endings allow time in relation to the length of therapy, sometimes weeks, sometimes many months, to consider, reflect upon and to mourn the end of the music therapy.

Framework of Therapy: Psychodynamic Theory

It is well known that human beings have the potential to recognise and respond to each other's feelings. A mother not only hears her baby crying, but also experiences it as a communication of his needs. A baby alone cannot manage or contain difficult feelings such as hunger or anger, so he projects them into the mother through the expressive quality of his crying. She is then moved to respond in a way that the baby can understand, with food or comfort, thus ensuring the baby's survival. Brown and Peddar cite Darwin's theory that mammals possess the capacity 'to pick up non-verbal cues about the emotional state of fellow beings so as to be able to know whether they are friend or foe' (1991: 63–4). Psychodynamic theory works on the principle that we repeat aspects of our earliest relationships, particularly those with our parents, throughout our adult life. Such repetition may become particularly evident within close relationships or relationships to authority figures. Psychotherapy makes use of the concepts of *Transference* and *Countertransference*. Transference refers to the transferring of feelings from an earlier relationship, usually with a parent, to one in the present. For example, in the workplace, where hierarchies of organisational structures may closely mirror family life, the most intense feelings can be activated. A manager who seems always too busy to take enough notice of a particular employee could be experienced as a distracted parent figure. This could connect to the employee's position in their own family in relation to a preoccupied parent. Psychotherapy uses this phenomenon, transference, to explore past, unconscious ways of relating and bring them to consciousness. The safe and confidential psychotherapeutic setting, in which the therapist reveals little information about themselves, allows a client to develop a transference relationship which can be gradually understood by both parties. The therapist's conscious and unconscious response to the client's transference is known as *Countertransference*. In music therapy, the therapist's experience of and response to the client's music may also be thought of as countertransference.

In Felipe's therapy, Rachel played and responded to him easily and creatively at first, but in the third session felt unable to play, except in a tense and restricted way. There was no apparent reason why this might be so – she was the same music therapist as before and had not lost her musical skill. She had not forgotten how to respond to Felipe in music, but instead was reacting to what he was communicating through his musical presence. She perceived through the musical countertransference his powerful need to keep her at a safe distance. In the case studies of both Felipe and Paul, the therapists' awareness of the therapeutic frame had an effect on the progress of the therapy, particularly in relation to keeping the boundaries of time. Response to the non-musical elements in the sessions were also significant – Paul's crying and Felipe's 'heaviness' both produced emotional responses in the therapists to which they needed to pay attention and could be understood as countertransference. Such understanding, though, as the case material indicates, is not a simple matter of cause and effect. How the therapists respond through their own feelings involves a process of self-learning, initially undertaken through training and personal therapy, and subsequently through clinical supervision. In Chapter 4 we will turn to the matter of training and resources for on-going clinical work. We shall see how the training that music therapists must undergo equips them to face the musical, emotional and psychological situations which they will meet in their daily work.

4

TRAINING AND SURVIVAL

'A musical experience needs three human beings at least. It requires a composer, a performer, and a listener: unless these three take part together there is no musical experience ... it demands as much effort on the listener's part as the other two corners of the triangle, this holy triangle of composer, performer and listener.'

Words spoken by Benjamin Britten,
on receiving the first Aspen Award, 31 July 1964.

The performance of live music is an intense interaction between musician and listener. Not only are the musician's communicative skills necessary to convey the essence of the music, but the particular quality of listening in an audience also affects the performer and the performance. Penelope Gouk suggests that 'any musician is potentially a healer, almost anywhere. This is because even just listening to music – for example in the concert hall, in the privacy of one's own home, or even a hospital ward – is often experienced as therapeutic' (2000: 11).

So musicians may frequently experience the potential of their chosen art form to be a healing agent, whether or not they develop an interest in music therapy. Although, judging from the large numbers of musicians who apply to do courses in music therapy, there is no shortage of individuals wishing to pursue it as a career, not everyone will want to follow a formal training. Some musicians are already employed within community organisations which offer support, such as centres for asylum seekers or refugees. They can also be found working in schools, hospitals or prisons, in units for young offenders and with drug or alcohol addicts. They may be sharing their musical skills with people who have had little opportunity to explore their musicality previously. Here the function of the music may be seen from different perspectives depending on whether the ethos of the setting is educational, recreational, artistic and/or therapeutic. Some settings, whilst therapeutic in intent, may deliberately avoid creating a therapeutic framework from within which to offer artistic activity. Instead of setting up a healer–patient relationship, they allow the opportunity for active engagement with the art form to be therapeutic in itself. The playwright David Hare describes his own experience when writing about the process of making the film *Paris by Night*:

> A profound and lasting contentment came upon me in that room, and it persisted through the remaining weeks of shooting. For as long as we worked, the process of art did what it has always promised: it comforted, it clarified, and set everything in order. ... this was one of the happiest times of my life. (1988: ix)

Community setting, such as a social services day centre, may offer a therapeutic approach* and while the music-making might begin with an artistic or recreational purpose, the emotional needs of the client often become a priority. These needs might be identified through the client's difficulty in relating to others in a group, or through disruptive or challenging behaviour. If, in these circumstances, such musicians find themselves becoming interested in working in more depth with a problem a client presents, they may consider music therapy training. Others may be more interested in aiming to facilitate that same client to participate in the music-making for its own sake and might be more drawn to attending music workshop or community music courses, some of which are offered at music colleges and universities.

At this point we are going to examine the process of becoming a music therapist. We will look at who can apply, what training will be offered, and why. Finally we will see how music therapists develop their work and how they gain deeper understanding of their patients and clients through the process of supervision.

What do Music Therapy Training Courses Demand?

1 Musicianship
The career leaflet published by the Association of Professional Music Therapists (APMT) states that, in order to become a music therapist,

---

*The Authors are indebted to musicians attending adult education classes at Birkbeck College, University of London, and Goldsmiths College, University of London, during 1996–2000, who have shared their working experiences, both verbally and through written work, and so informed this view.

an undergraduate degree in music or evidence of training in music at a professional level is required. It is this stipulation which members of the public most frequently question when enquiring about music therapy training. Why is it necessary to have musical *qualifications*? Does this mean that the profession will not consider amongst its applicants self-taught musicians or people whose professional playing has never involved the taking of examinations?

In reality, defining musical ability in the context of training to be a music therapist is chiefly about a musician's own relationship to music. Applicants to music therapy courses come from a wide variety of backgrounds which include teaching, social work, psychology and medicine in addition to music performance. When coming to audition the most important consideration will not be how many exams they have passed or competitions they have won, but rather the way in which they relate to their main instrument. The audition panel will be looking, first and foremost, for *communication*. Does the music speak, and does the listener feel that something about the player is being communicated through their playing? Does the player respond sensitively to, for example, the piano accompanist? Other aspects of an applicant's playing will include demonstration of a *commitment* to their first instrument, through evidence of technical skill gained over many years. Another attribute essential to becoming a music therapist is *flexibility*. In addition to playing pre-prepared music, can the player improvise in response to another player? Do they listen to what another might play and respond in the moment? Can they use their voice to sing expressively, even if they might never have had formal training? Of prime importance, music therapists need to feel 'at home' in playing music. It needs to be an integral part of them, both in terms of what they do in their lives and as a natural means of self-expression. This is a relationship which a formal training with a certificate can suggest but never guarantee.

The music therapy training is designed to equip competent musicians to use their music for therapeutic purposes. This can be a difficult experience for many students, who are used to performing or teaching, and although much self-doubt may be experienced in both these activities, nevertheless a clear task is involved, which to a great extent has a clear outcome. In music therapy the task is sometimes clear but the outcome can rarely be predicted. Much of the training in music therapy focuses on learning how to improvise, not just in the music, but as part of communicating with another person. The music therapy student has to learn to experience a sense of failure, not due to a lack of technique or musicality, but because the musical relationship in music therapy normally takes a considerable time and great patience on the part of both therapist and client. This can result in a sense of loss of skill and musical potency in some students. Even for the skilled improviser, for example a jazz musician, it is no longer enough to be able to respond freely to the music of another in the moment. The music therapist learns to respond to both the client and their music (which is part of them) all at once. The process of clinical improvisation, and the difference between improvisation and clinical improvisation which the music therapy student gradually assimilates, is at the heart of the music therapy student's process of learning.

2   Personal Suitability

Traditionally, in many forms of healing or medicine, the personality of the therapist or healer has been an integral part of the healing process. In the folk medicine tradition of sixteenth-century England, charms or incantations were sometimes used to accompany the dispensing of medicine. Their success depended upon the special qualities of the healer, in addition to the properties of the medicament itself. The origin of the word 'charm' provides an insight into this expectation, as it has its roots in the Latin word *carmen*, meaning incantation or enchantment (Hoad, 1996: 71). It may not be surprising that 'charm' eventually came to refer to personality as well as to the method of healing. By the seventeenth century it was being used to mean 'attractive quality', and today the same word refers to 'the power or quality of giving delight' (*Concise Oxford Dictionary*, 1991: 189). Music therapy places intense personal demands upon the therapist, since to work with the inner world of a client involves a commitment to engaging with one's inner self. Clients come to music therapy with emotional and psychological issues which may resonate with issues in the therapist's own life. For this reason, therapists have to work very hard to understand themselves, their conflicts and ways of relating. Audition panels need to ascertain the psychological health of potential students and their level of personal insight. Prospective trainees need to be motivated to engage in the process of self-learning and to meet with and confront their own areas of defence and vulnerability. How can we work with the defences and vulnerabilities of our clients if we have no knowledge of these aspects of ourselves? Mércèdes Pavlicevic writes personally of her process of becoming a therapist:

When I began to work with profoundly and multiply handicapped people in Scotland, I had overwhelming feelings of nausea and exhaustion, and was frequently ill. I then met my first 'violent' patient, a 'crazy' young woman of mild mental handicap. I was paralysed with fear, certain that she would attack me at the earliest opportunity. Of course, at the time I saw that all the 'violence' was in the patient: safely out there, somewhere, away from me ... As the healer, I was unable to tolerate my own inner wounds and needed to keep them tightly stitched. 'Mad' people could 'play out' my own madness for me, out there and I could remain 'sane' – although I paid the price somatically. (1997: 179–80)

Pavlicevic writes further of the psychological work she needed to do in order to deepen her work, and to relieve some of the inner stress involved in persistently projecting difficult parts of herself into her patients:

It is interesting that it is now, many years later, that I am filled with doubts about my clinical work: I wonder for instance, who is being the therapist and who is being the client; I recognise that I need music therapy – and indeed if I do not practice for any length of time, I miss it: the intensity, dynamism, directness: these are my needs, coupled with needing to be valued, to be seen as helping. (1997: 180)

All the music therapy training courses in the UK stipulate that 'evidence of maturity and stability is required' and the state regulatory body further requires applicants to be at least 23 years of age. In the same way that prospective trainees need flexible, reflective and expressive musicianship, they also need flexible, reflective and expressive personalities – an openness to change and growth of both musicianship and personality is vital in order to do the work.

3   Intellectual Curiosity

Although engaging in the experiential study of music therapy through clinical practice is central to training, equally crucial is the ability to learn about the work from an objective and academic stance. Students must learn how to employ the body of music therapy knowledge which has been built up over the last 40 years and, where relevant, how to access information and ideas from other disciplines such as psychology, psychotherapy, medicine, philosophy and musicology. It is also crucial to be able to learn about the clients from the perspective of the problems or pathology which they present. Knowing about the effects of dementia, for example, will enable the music therapist to have a fuller understanding of the client's needs and how music therapy might help. Similarly, such knowledge is essential for the therapist to be able to communicate with other professionals, both discursively and in the writing of reports. The acquisition of academic skills during training is not only to facilitate more fluent reading and writing but also to develop a habit of thinking critically about clinical work and developing the potential for holding in mind more than one point of view at a time. Students are required to write case studies or dissertations about their clinical work which will not only reflect on what happened musically, but show analytical skills in processing the material and setting it within a relevant theoretical framework.

What Happens During Training?

At the time of writing, the entry requirement to the profession is by way of a postgraduate diploma in music therapy. It is anticipated that eventually all programmes will be at Masters level, so that entry to the profession and to state registration will be based on successful completion of a Masters degree.

The training courses in the UK have agreed the following Mission Statement to reflect the shared aims of all the courses:

> To train musicians in clinical, professional and musical skills, giving the necessary medical, psychological and practical knowledge in order to practise music therapy within health, education, social services and in the private sector. (APMT, 1997)

In order to fulfil these criteria, each course must undertake to equip the students with:

- musical skills and knowledge;
- therapy skills and knowledge;
- supportive medical and psychological studies;
- academic skills and an introduction to research;
- observation of music therapy;
- supervised clinical placements with at least two contrasting client groups; and
- personal growth through individual and group experiential sessions.

Exactly how these requirements are fulfilled will depend on the ethos of each individual course. While one may study a particular approach to music therapy in considerable depth, another may be more eclectic, drawing from a wide range of sources. There may be more time spent on placement in one training course, while another may schedule more practical improvisation sessions. Philosophical stances of the courses may also vary. For example, they might describe their approach as 'music centred' or 'humanistic and person-centred' or 'psycho-dynamic'. As long as each course meets the requirements that have been agreed between the profession and the state regulatory body, the Health Professions Council, there is freedom for each course to maintain its individuality. Quality and standards are ensured by regular academic and statutory reviews and by having external examiners who moderate the ongoing assessment procedures of the internal teams of tutors. For detailed up-to-date information regarding music therapy training courses in the UK, see the British Society for Music Therapy website: www.bsmt.org

What Happens After Training?

Training to be a professional music therapist presents demands and challenges, but the work itself brings many rewards. In common with other professions however, it also has the potential to feel repetitive and to lose its sense of challenge, so that practitioners may come to feel a loss of interest or lack of motivation for their work. This might be connected to the struggle that many therapists experience in maintaining the status of a music therapy service as a clinically effective and financially viable form of treatment. This can occur particularly in a hierarchical environment where each profession has its place, based upon the age-old tension between science and the humanities, or between a medical and a holistic model. In such a setting, music therapists may experience isolation and low self-esteem, making it hard to feel positive or creative about their work.

In addition, the perpetual demands of the work require the music therapist to engage with the emotional needs of others, and this in itself can be physically and emotionally draining. For therapists to work with the process of change in a client, they have to be able to engage with the part of themselves that is also able to change. We believe that it is impossible for the working therapist to survive over a period of years without using resources which nurture an engagement between their own creativity and their clinical work.

Musical Resources
We believe that an active interest in music, whether through performing, composing or listening, is essential for this work. To engage

with live music and to hear or create new sounds, feeds the part of oneself that responds to the clients in music. To listen to music or to learn new music to play or to perform is to find out something new about one's own instrument, and helps to maintain the technical flexibility and musical expressiveness which facilitates responses from clients. Free improvisation, in a non-clinical setting, can also enable development of one's own 'musical thinking'. Where groups of music therapists work together, this can be experienced as enormously satisfying, on a number of different levels, not least that of bringing colleagues closer together.

Continuing Professional Development (CPD)

Music therapists, along with other healthcare professionals, are required by law to maintain their skills after training by undertaking regular CPD. This can take many different forms, including private study, reading and research or writing articles, lectures and presentations for conferences. Developing musical skills or studying other areas related to music therapy are also options. The writing of this book, for example, has involved a creative mixture of emotional and intellectual processes which in turn has offered new insights to our clinical work. A team of music therapists working together at a hospital set themselves the task of regularly listening to tapes of clinical improvisations from each other's sessions. The project afforded professional development in areas such as listening skills, talking about music for clinical purposes, and heightening awareness of the many possible varieties of musical interaction. These are all ways of stimulating, renewing and advancing a personal interest in music therapy as a clinical skill and as a discipline for study.

Personal Development

Undertaking personal therapy is a requirement for everyone training to be a music therapist. It can take the form of psychotherapy, counselling, or one of the arts therapies, including music therapy. Personal therapy, however, relates to a process of self-learning which is not just confined to training and is potentially life-long. Undertaking therapy on a long-term basis affords the possibility of containment and reflection, in addition to the exploration of painful feelings and much hard psychological work. It is sometimes surprising for the lay-person to learn that therapists might undertake their own therapy, and for some this might provide a disincentive to train. Such a process, however, enables greater awareness of oneself in relation to others and of the effect we may have on other people, and of some of the unconscious disturbances which block or upset our relationships. An experience of active engagement with our own emotional world enables a far greater active engagement with our patients, and is crucial, we believe, to maintaining interest in their emotional world. Additionally, the music therapist is often working on the fringes of organisations and, as we have indicated, often needs great determination in order to survive. Organisations, with their culture of hierarchy and authority figures, are rich in parallels with the relationships in family life. Personal therapy can enable the therapist to understand how some of these ways of relating may be derived from the past, which can in turn be very helpful in dealing with the daily problems of work. Some of these organisational conflicts may also be understood and supported from within supervision.

Supervision
'Supervision' is derived from the Latin words *super* (over) and *videre* (to see), giving the meaning 'to oversee' (Hoad, 1996: 173). Dileo describes supervision as 'at the foundation of promoting professional growth in music therapy', not only through its role of teaching students how 'to practice music therapy competently and ethically', but also in improving and enhancing the skills of working music therapists (2001: 19).

In 2000, UK government legislation made it mandatory for all healthcare professionals to receive supervision on a regular basis. It has therefore become a professional requirement for music therapists, not just whilst studying or at the beginning of their careers, but throughout their working lives. The purpose of this legislation was to provide a means of regulating the quality of care that patients were receiving and, in particular, to minimise the likelihood of medical errors. While music therapy supervision also has a role in ensuring the protection of the public, it focuses primarily on the heart of the work, the therapeutic relationship developed through the music.

Supervision undertaken within any profession will normally entail a regular meeting between the clinician and a senior colleague to discuss aspects of the supervisee's work, focusing either on clinical or managerial issues, or a combination of both. In music therapy supervision, the supervisee will generally take material from a clinical session to the supervisor, in the form of written notes along with an audio or video tape recording of the session. Brown describes one of the aims of music therapy supervision as being 'holding and containment for the supervisee and client dyad' (1997: 4). She refers to Casement's concept of the 'nursing triad' (1985: 27) in which a mother needs another adult to hold and support her in the relationship with her child, 'especially in situations where the child feels unmanageable, or where feelings of inadequacy or guilt arise for the mother' (Brown, 1997: 4) This makes clear the primarily supportive function of supervision, and while supervisees may at times feel inadequate or exposed in presenting their work, the stance of the supervisor should be essentially non-judgemental.

Brown (1997: 5) suggests five areas of concern which commonly arise in music therapy supervision:

1 Musical relationship in the therapy room.
2 Practical management in the therapy room and workplace.
3 Interpersonal dynamics in the therapy room.
4 Interpersonal dynamics in the workplace.
5 Interpersonal dynamics in the supervision room.

Any of these categories may need to be addressed and given more or less attention at different times, depending on the experience and specific needs of the supervisee. As well as listening to and discussing the clinical material and the feelings evoked by it, some supervisors may also engage in practical musical role-play with the supervisee, while others may recommend reading material and discuss theoretical ideas.

The following case study is written from the perspective of Ellen, a newly-qualified music therapist, and is based around the type of clinical experiences which may be brought to supervision by a therapist at the beginning of a career.

Case Study: Ellen

Before training as a music therapist, Ellen had been a music teacher, working in schools with children of all ages. Although she had enjoyed many aspects of teaching, she found that behaviour management was an ongoing problem, as every class seemed to contain at least one pupil who was determined to disrupt the music lesson with boisterous or uncooperative behaviour. Ellen wanted the children to enjoy music, so she was reluctant to raise her voice or even to be firm, so that sometimes the lessons contained a certain amount of chaos. This left her frequently feeling out of control and worried about her effectiveness as a teacher. When she changed her career, however, and became a music therapist, Ellen felt she had found her vocation.

In her first job she worked with non-verbal children and adults with profound and multiple disabilities whose responses to the music she improvised were both encouraging and inspiring. Despite the slow rate of change and development, Ellen felt that she was making a real contact with the clients and that she was able to use music as therapy. Her supervision at this time focused on helping her to listen more acutely and critically to the shared musical improvisations and to find ways of matching her clients' sounds more accurately and directly.

In her second year of work, Ellen was referred a new client, an 8-year-old boy called Frankie. As a young child at nursery school, Frankie's disturbed, anti-social behaviour and his poor concentration led to his parents seeking medical and psychological help for him. He was diagnosed as having Attention Deficit Hyperactivity Disorder (ADHD) and was put on a course of medication. The treatment was not successful; Frankie had an adverse reaction to the drug, becoming even more disturbed and aggressive, so the medication was withdrawn. Frankie's parents were given advice by a psychologist on how to manage his behaviour, but it showed little sign of improving. Despite having average intelligence, he was failing academically, being unable to read or write. Mainstream primary schools could not cope with him and he was even excluded from the special school to which he had been moved. At the time of his referral to music therapy, his parents were waiting for him to be allocated a place in a therapeutic boarding school for children with similar problems, but meanwhile he had no schooling and was showing increasingly difficult behaviour at home. His safety was a real issue, as he had no sense of danger – his mother said that he would run out of the house and straight across the busy main road if she did not keep the doors locked. In desperation, his parents brought him to the music therapy centre where Ellen worked, as they had read that music therapy was an effective treatment for children with all kinds of problems. Following a process of assessment Ellen accepted the challenge and began to work with him.

In his first session Frankie was very excited to see the music room and the instruments and played them all, with vigour and dexterity, extremely loudly. Ellen noticed that he did not stay with any instrument for more than a few seconds and that he was rarely still. He asked her many questions, which made Ellen uneasy, but he did not wait to hear the answers. Halfway through the session, Frankie suddenly ran out of the door and was halfway along the corridor before Ellen realised what was happening. It was then impossible to persuade him to come back to the music room as he had begun playing with the toys in the waiting room.

When the second session came, a week later, Frankie was eager to get started but after ten minutes he seemed to have exhausted all the possibilities of making music in a conventional way. He began to gather the instruments up and took them behind the piano where Ellen could not see him. A moment later a tambourine flew through the air 'like a boomerang', Frankie shouted excitedly, followed by a metal chime bar which narrowly missed Ellen's head. She began to feel anxious and out of control as Frankie then ran round the room, whooping and knocking everything over. She asked him politely to calm down and then began to play some soothing music on the piano, but Frankie took no notice. After a few more minutes, Ellen decided to end the session early.

In supervision with an experienced colleague, Lydia, Ellen gave an animated and graphic description of the difficult session, saying that she dreaded the next meeting with Frankie and had no idea what she would do with him. Instead of instantly giving helpful advice, Lydia listened in silence as Ellen poured out the story, and then asked what her feelings had been during the session. After a pause, Ellen admitted that she had felt a sense of failure in not being able to 'manage' Frankie, that she was letting him and his parents down, and that her own weaknesses were now being truly exposed. She had also felt unsafe in the room with him, wondering if he might hurt her, even unintentionally. Lydia asked her if the feelings she was describing reminded her of anything she had experienced previously. Ellen then began to reminisce about her life as a teacher, and how she had sometimes despaired of 'getting through' to the most difficult pupils. 'I thought I had left all that behind when I finished teaching,' she sighed. It was becoming apparent to Ellen that the 'unfinished business' from her former career and the feelings of inadequacy which she had experienced then were emerging again in her work with Frankie. Lydia asked her how she thought Frankie might have felt during the session. Ellen then realised that in naming her own feelings she had also been discovering something important about her client. Like her, Frankie was struggling with unmanageable and out-of-control feelings; like her, he was experiencing a sense of failure, and perhaps he, too, felt unsafe in the therapy room and afraid of his own potential for violence. Ellen and Lydia thought together about practical ways in which the therapy room could be made to feel safer for client and therapist, and how clear boundaries needed to be set, to protect them both and to preserve the therapeutic space.

Lydia then asked Ellen if she could hear the audio recording of the session to see how the music contributed to the developing situation. They listened to the part of the session where things had begun to become difficult. At first, Frankie could be heard drumming energetically, while Ellen matched his playing with strong, lively music on the piano. There was a gradual accelerando (speeding up) in Frankie's drumming, leading to some chaotic and uncontrolled beating which ended abruptly with him throwing the sticks away. Then his voice could be heard becoming increasingly shrill and excitable, as he threw the other instruments and ran around the room. Meanwhile, Ellen's piano playing was becoming ever slower, softer and more tentative, and eventually faded out altogether. Her voice, when she spoke, sounded unsure and apologetic. The musical empathy which she had shown at the beginning of the session had vanished, and she was no longer able to meet Frankie, either musically or emotionally. Listening to the tape, Ellen could hear that her music had not 'held' Frankie at the moment of his accelerando. It was as though she had abandoned him because he had become too 'difficult', and neither had she been unable to set clear boundaries, musically or verbally, which would have enabled the musical exchange to have continued. Lydia and Ellen discussed musical techniques which she could use in order to provide stronger music, capable of containing Frankie's chaotic playing. It was also important for Ellen to monitor how she spoke to Frankie, so that her voice could be firm and therefore reassuring, without becoming authoritarian.

At first, in this unfamiliar area of music therapy work, Ellen needed much support and encouragement from Lydia. She also used her ongoing personal psychotherapy sessions to explore some of the uncomfortable feelings which had arisen in relation to Frankie, issues which she found connected to her childhood. As time went on, Ellen was able to understand on an emotional level what Lydia had said to her, and could therefore become, to some extent, her own supervisor, both during the sessions and when listening to the tapes afterwards. This then freed her supervision time to discuss other clients who needed her attention.

We began this chapter with a three-sided musical relationship and have finished with another: the client, the therapist and supervisor. In the chapters that follow we will look at clinical work in greater detail.

PART II

Clinical Matters

5

IMPROVISATION

The word 'improvise' comes from the Latin *improvisus* meaning 'unforeseen'. In music therapy the therapist creates an environment of experimentation to allow the emergence of unforeseen musical material. This kind of improvisation does not only happen in music. Casement (1985: 3) has emphasised the importance for the therapist of 'not knowing' in psychoanalysis. To think that one knows what it is the patient needs to make him or her 'better' or to foresee what will happen in the therapy immediately creates a presumption about the patient, and so may blind the therapist to what the patient is trying to communicate. Close to this way of working is the technique central to psychoanalysis – that of free association.

Improvisation in Music Therapy and Free Association

Freud discovered in his consulting room that far more could be learned about the emotional make-up of his clients by encouraging them to 'freely associate', that is, to say whatever came into their minds rather than by direct questioning. Freud developed this method, postulating that if a patient expressed what was on his mind without repressing it, he would eventually come to talk about what was really significant, however obscure or random the contents of his private thoughts might appear to be. In the trusting environment of the analytic session, patients would begin to reveal thoughts and fantasies that they would normally keep from others and even hide from their conscious selves. The task of the analyst was to try to understand this material, or to make interpretations about what it might mean. Freud's investigations also led him to realise that it was not just the patient's thoughts and fantasies which were of significance. Much could also be learnt about a patient's unconscious world from observing and understanding the relationship that developed between the analyst and the patient.

The technique of free improvisation as used by music therapists has direct parallels to free association, as we believe that in improvising the client is presenting a self-portrait in music and that, through the shared musical interaction, a therapeutic relationship can be gradually formed.

In the case example that follows, John's improvisation created a very particular atmosphere in the therapy room.

Case Study: John

John, a 75-year-old Londoner, had a mild brain injury as a result of a car accident in his youth. He was becoming increasingly dependent upon alcohol, and his relationship with his daughter, who lived close by, was deteriorating as he became more and more demanding. John was a long-term patient in a day hospital for older adults where he attended a music therapy group over a two-year period. On one occasion, after he had been in the group for about a year, he was the only group member to arrive. The music therapist decided to work with him on his own, rather than cancel the session. John arranged two drums, a metallophone and a cymbal around him, and proceeded to play each in turn over and over again, producing a slow rhythmic sequence. The therapist played the piano to support John's playing, providing a steady pulse and experimenting with different accompaniments. She created a melody by playing random single notes and added some simple rhythmic patterns. The therapist was trying to make a musical connection with John, or at least reassure him that he was in a safe place and that his music could be heard. She was also providing a musical invitation for him to join in with her music. This she did by playing sounds that afforded the possibility of interaction – such as a regular pulse, and later by introducing some more formed music in the style of an Irish jig. As the session continued, however, the therapist's experience of being with John was one of being unable to make any connection at all. She felt that he was very isolated and desolate and that he had presented this part of himself in his music. In the group setting his isolation had to some extent been concealed, but alone with the therapist his inability to be interactive or communicative was starkly revealed. This new understanding of John enabled the therapist to identify some of his needs and the future direction the work might take.

Clinical Improvisation in Music Therapy and John Cage

As we have seen in previous chapters, music therapists hear all sounds in the music therapy room as having the potential to inspire a musical response, even if such sounds are jangled, chaotic or made on objects other than musical instruments. That it is possible to conceptualise music in such a broad way can be attributed in part to certain musical developments in America and Europe in the last century. The American experimental composer John Cage might be considered an important, if curious, influence. During the 1930s he expounded a radical notion of music. He proclaimed that all sounds had equal status and therefore had the potential to be part of a piece of music. This was irrespective of whether the sounds could be written down or whether or not they were created upon a musical instrument. These ideas were evolved from Cage's conviction that the future of music would be defined by the new technological possibilities created by electronic music. Cage wrote:

> The special function of electrical instruments will be to provide complete control of the overtone structure of tones (as opposed to noises) and to make these tones available in any frequency, amplitude and duration which will make available for musical purposes any and all sounds that can be heard. (1958: 4)

The music therapist similarly makes use of all sounds which are available, in particular those that the player can create without any technical skill. This is one reason why percussion instruments are essential tools in the work.

Cage wrote that 'Any sound is acceptable to the composer of percussion music; he explores the academically forbidden "non-musical" field of sound insofar as is manually possible' (1958: 4). He encouraged twentieth-century musicians and audiences to open their ears and to listen in a musical way to the sounds around them, whatever those might be. We can see how this links to improvisational approaches to music therapy and how it has contributed to us arriving in the twenty-first century, willing to hear any sound or collection of sounds as music.

Alvin commented on this at the outset of music therapy in Britain when she wrote:

> Music therapy benefits from the fact that musical means are becoming richer and more available to us all. Musicians use new techniques unthought of some years ago. Contemporary composers of the avant-garde act as explorers in a world of sounds and often provide us with strange experiences related to the modern scene. (1974: 105)

73

Alvin linked this freedom in playing music to a freedom of psychological expression that might emerge within the music therapy setting. She writes, 'In the process [that is, the music therapy process] the patient can overcome his self-consciousness, his sense of fear and reveal an untouched side of his inner life' (1974: 105).

In the following case vignette the therapist was influenced by a performance of Cage's *Musicircus* that she had recently attended. The programme notes described *Musicircus* as 'an event inspired by Cage's radical views of contemporary aesthetic and social issues ... music emanating from unexpected places and unexpected spaces. A chaos of sound awaiting your discovery as music.' (Montague, 1998).

The setting is a mental health day hospital where a music therapy session is taking place with a group of elderly clients who have senile dementia. The clients in the group are called Doris, Michael, Frank, Edith and Joe. They have attended group music therapy over a period of 18 months, over which time they gradually found they could express much feeling through their music-making. They frequently expressed surprise both at this experience and at the fact that they felt able to share thoughts and experiences which otherwise would have been quite private. At the start of one session, soon after they had begun attending the group, the therapist, Rachel, invited each group member to choose an instrument. She then picked up a drum to play herself, but waited first to hear and see what was happening in the room. Joe, shaking the maracas, Edith, playing the xylophone and Frank, who was beating a tambour, were all playing different rhythms and at different speeds. At the same time Doris was anxiously asking the nurse, Monica, where she had left her coat, while Michael was looking through a box of percussion instruments which jangled and rattled. Before Rachel could begin to play, Joe had stopped playing and was asking her the name of his instrument. Rachel had to decide how to respond. She could either wait and not play herself until the coat had been found and people were settled, or she could start to play her drum in such a way that people might be drawn in and gradually begin to settle. Either way might have helped the group to begin.

In fact, what Rachel actually found herself doing was starting to play in direct response to the different sounds being created in the room and the slightly chaotic atmosphere. She imitated

the jangles and rattles, and sang answers to the questions
about the instruments and the concerns about the lost coat. She
did this to communicate to the clients that all the sounds in the
room had been heard, in a musical way, and were part of the
session, not just the sounds which might be played convention-
ally on the musical instruments.

It can be seen from this example that improvisation does not just take place in the playing of music in music therapy. The therapist improvises all of his or her responses to the clients, including the decision about whether, when or how to play.

What Music is Improvised in Music Therapy?

Music therapists are commonly asked what music they use, and yet this is an impossible question to answer. They have available to them as a therapeutic tool all that music as a medium has been or can be, so that with any one patient or any group of clients there is a vast potential in the variety of musical sounds that could be made. As we have seen, students training to become music therapists in Britain are taught techniques of improvisation. They also learn to listen acutely to their patients and to attune to the improvised music that they make. However, in keeping with the improvised nature of a music therapy relationship, music therapists are not working from a premise that a prescribed type of sound or style is required for a certain type of patient. Instead, they intuitively use whatever musical sounds or musical resources seem to be appropriate for a particular patient in that moment. In the same way that we develop conversational formulae or 'small-talk' to ease an initial meeting or a social situation, so music therapists develop a personal repertoire of ways to start a musical conversation. The music improvised by a music therapy beginner can sometimes sound a little like a tourist using a foreign language who takes a sentence straight out of the phrase book but then is not able to develop the conversation further. The beginner music therapist might invite the patient to play, who then bangs loudly on the drum, to which the music therapist responds with a single sound, also on a drum. Then there is an awkward silence. In both scenarios, something has been initiated, but the possibility of its continuation is limited by neither tourist nor therapist knowing what to say next.

Sutton has written about the significance of silence, comparing its roles in music and in conversation. She writes:

> The term *silence* is used here in a form that is relative to sound, rather than the scientific definition; silence is seen as an absence of musical sound and not absolute silence (such as that existing in outer space). *Silence* in music begins with the space before the first musical sound begins and ends with the space after the last musical sound has finished. ... Both natural conversation and free musical improvisation are made up of sound and silence. (2001: 106)

Sutton goes on to say that while silence has an important structural role, it can also be the cause of discomfort when it occurs in conversation, and extended silence can lead to the breakdown of the interaction (2001: 106–19). Sutton found, however, that 'In music, the situation is more flexible,' so that pauses or silences are of great structural importance in creating or relieving tension, attracting attention and drawing the listener in, and do not generally cause the music to disintegrate.

Sound and Silence: Two Clinical Examples

We can see in the following case examples that the therapist experienced the silence of her clients during the improvisations in two very different ways.

Thomas was a man in his early forties with mild learning difficulties, attending music therapy for only the second time. As he played tentatively on the xylophone, it seemed to the music therapist as though the long silences between his random notes were as significant as the sounds themselves. The therapist also played random sounds and left silences, in reply. She did not attempt to fill in the gaps or to provide any more musical structure, beyond the framework of 'question and answer'.

Sheila, a woman in her late seventies with Alzheimer's disease, was meeting Rachel, the music therapist, for the first time. She chose a drum and began to play, accompanied by Rachel on the cello. Rachel noticed that if she (the therapist) made any pauses or brief silences in her music, Sheila would also stop playing, looking at her anxiously. It seemed that she needed to be accompanied all the time to feel confident enough to play. After some experimenting, Rachel began to play a continuous,

slow walking rhythm, rather like a ground bass, in the tempo
of Sheila's playing. This simple repetitive musical structure
enabled Sheila to feel confident enough to continue with her
playing and gradually to experiment with the different sounds
she could make on the drum.

As musicians, music therapists bring their own musical experiences,
preferences and skills to their work and will draw upon a deeply
rooted 'autobiography' of music. This inner autobiography will be
made up of significant pieces of music, musical experiences and
moments of performance, which will carry personal meaning.
Together with a psychological capacity for forming a therapeutic
relationship and an ability to learn about unfamiliar music from the
client, this musical repertoire of skills and experiences forms the
basis of the music therapist's tool kit. As music therapists become
more experienced, they become more adept at dipping into it for the
musical tools required, in response to the patient. It is not surprising, therefore, that many music therapists speak of their relationship with music changing as their experience of therapy deepens.
They begin to listen to musical performances in a concert hall, or in
other settings, in a much freer and more receptive way, finding
themselves able to appreciate a far greater range of musical styles.
Many speak of their own playing changing, becoming more attuned
to other players, and freer in their range of musical expression.
Nordoff and Robbins wrote:

> The therapist may be musically very knowledgeable, he may have
> performed often, or have composed much music, yet now music becomes
> revitalized for him, completely changed in purpose and realization. All the
> compositional styles evolved during the last seven centuries, all the folk
> music, the idioms, the elements of music, the very notes themselves –
> even the smallest expressive and structural components – become signif-
> icant in countless, undreamed of ways. The world of music opens anew,
> now disclosing an inner musical life of therapeutic potential. The thera-
> pist feels reborn in his new musical-therapeutic experiences and realizes
> that the art of music will never cease to challenge him, never cease to
> require all his musical resources. (1992: 142)

This still leaves the dilemma, though, of what sort of music should
occur – is there a right or wrong? If music therapists are taught to
improvise as the central technique in therapy, what happens if the
patient wants to sing a popular song, or an autistic child plays the
same rhythm on the same drum each week? The therapist has to

find a musical way to respond and might wonder, in the first case, whether to go to the piano and suggest a song to the patient, or wait for the patient to start singing or simply start to hum some sounds. In the second example, should the therapist match the child's perseverative drum beating exactly, or provide an alternative experience by playing in a different tempo or metre? There *is* no correct answer, of course. There is no *right* response beyond that which feels right in a particular moment with a particular patient, and within the context of the therapeutic goals for that individual. However, as Nordoff and Robbins indicate above, there are many musical resources that the music therapist can turn to which may well guide them to the place where the client is able to communicate. Melodies can be diatonic, pentatonic, atonal or modal; texture can be in a single line, polyphonic or chordal; harmony may be chromatic, romantic or dissonant, and the therapist may employ such musical idioms as jazz, pop, blues, rap and soul as well as styles derived from classical music. Musical structures, which include songs, rondos, 'call and response', ostinati and ternary form, can be used according to the amount of support or direction, musical or non-musical, that a client needs in any one moment.

Two Examples of the Use of Specific Musical Techniques

Diane Austin is a music therapist working in private practice with adult clients, many of whom 'have histories of emotional, physical and/or sexual abuse'. Austin uses 'a combination of improvised vocal music with verbal processing', relying on the strength of a simple harmonic structure to support her clients' improvising, through a technique which she has called 'vocal holding'. She writes:

> Vocal holding techniques involve creating a consistent and stable musical environment to facilitate spontaneity and emotional connection through the use of vocal improvisation. These techniques are not meant to be a 'prescription' … When I work with a client who is musically knowledgeable, I begin by asking what two chords he would like me to play. If he has little or no knowledge of chord structure, I play examples of major and minor chords and ask which sound he prefers. Sometimes a client describes a feeling or mood he would like to evoke and together we find the desired chords. I also ask the client if he would like a particular rhythm. This technique is usually limited to two chords in order to establish a predictable, secure, musical container in which the client does not have to think but can relax and allow his spontaneous self to emerge. The chord pattern is played repeatedly for the client to improvise over. (1998: 315–17)

Austin goes on to describe how the client can move from non-verbal singing, through mirroring (by the therapist) to harmonizing, and eventually into 'free associative singing' over the two-chord pattern in which the client can voice their feelings through 'a musical stream of consciousness' (1998: 320).

Robarts describes the use of similarly small motifs with her client, 11-year-old Tina. In this case, it was Tina herself who restricted the musical vocabulary of the session by repeatedly playing a two-note pattern, first on the marimba and then on the piano. Tina was an in-patient in a child and adolescent psychiatric unit, receiving treatment for anorexia nervosa and obsessive-compulsive disorder. Robarts interpreted Tina's rigid and restricted musical motif as being a symbol or metaphor which reflected 'her inflexibility and lack of spontaneity, her insecurity and inability to explore and be playful. Symbolically they seemed reminiscent of her rocking to induce vomiting, which she frequently did after mealtimes, as well as indicating emotional deficits in infancy due to her mother's depression' (1994: 11–13).

Robarts incorporated Tina's musical offering, the two-note theme, 'played either on the black notes, d flat and e flat or on the white notes, f and e natural,' into a variety of improvisations at the piano.

> My accompaniment to these improvisations always acknowledged that I valued her controlled musical 'morsels', which were reminiscent of the tiny pieces of apple that were the only form of solid food she would accept at mealtimes. ... By the fifth session, she had discovered that her two black notes were the beginning of a tune she knew and could pick out on the piano. It was the 'Skye Boat Song'. She wanted me to listen to her, then invited me to play too. I asked her what sort of music she wanted. 'Rocking music,' she said, 'like the sea under the boat.' 'You like to be rocked by the music.' Tina nodded and continued playing. (1994: 11–13)

This was the beginning of Tina being able to accept what the therapist had to offer, and so to enrich and build up her fragile self, both physically and emotionally.

From Structure to Improvisation: A Continuum

In addition to being a tool, the use of musical structures by therapist and client can also be seen as a manifestation of the musical relationship

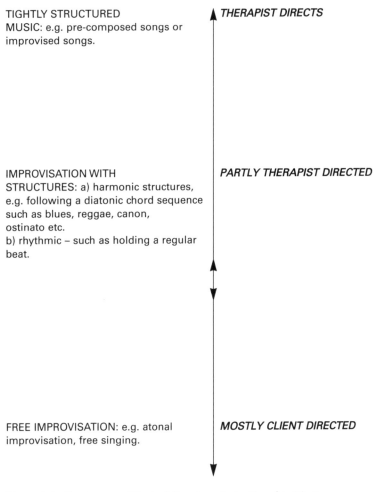

TIGHTLY STRUCTURED
MUSIC: e.g. pre-composed songs or
improvised songs.

THERAPIST DIRECTS

IMPROVISATION WITH
STRUCTURES: a) harmonic structures,
e.g. following a diatonic chord sequence
such as blues, reggae, canon,
ostinato etc.
b) rhythmic – such as holding a regular
beat.

PARTLY THERAPIST DIRECTED

FREE IMPROVISATION: e.g. atonal
improvisation, free singing.

MOSTLY CLIENT DIRECTED

Figure 5.1   *Continuum of Musical Structures to be Found in Music
Therapy*

at any given time. In this next section we will explore this idea in
some depth. Figure 5.1 depicts three different types of musical form –
free improvisation, structured improvisation and pre-composed
music – on a continuum which ranges from highly-structured to
freely-improvised music. The purpose of the diagram is to show how

all the musical experiences which can occur in a music therapy session are related. These musical possibilities might occur either:

- within a single session;
- over a period of time; or
- with specific clients.

Within A Single Session
In this case example the therapist consciously assists the group's music to progress from chaotic free improvisation to structured improvisation within one session.

In an adult mental health setting, the music of a new group of patients, who were acutely ill, was extremely chaotic. Some were playing music which was loud and energetic, whilst others were quietly experimenting with a drum or acoustic guitar, sitting in the corner, almost unheard. The therapist felt an urgent need to provide some structure. She began to play a simple three chord progression on the piano, at first starting with single notes, and then gradually building up the chords so that they became more complex, whilst keeping the same simple three chord pattern. She used the sounds she was making as a means of providing a musical focus, a point of safety, leadership, and containment. It was as though she was a mother putting down a large mat in a nursery upon which all the children could play together. Gradually the patients' sounds became less disparate and more connected as they began to respond to the security of the musical structure that the therapist was providing.

Over a Period of Time
In the following case example we see how the therapist responded to a man who brought his own personal music to the sessions, in the form of songs, and how his use of these song structures changed over a period of time.

Winston was an elderly man of 73 who was referred to a day hospital for an assessment of his cognitive and emotional state. He lived in a hostel for homeless West Indian men where the workers were very concerned about him, particularly as they had not known him for very long and they wondered if he might have dementia. He seemed to have difficulty remembering his recent past, and frequently became lost if he went out alone. They described him as extremely isolated and vulnerable, with a tendency to become aggressive. Although he had much to say, it seemed as though he shut people out, and the day hospital staff found it difficult to talk to him about his needs, either practical or emotional, including trying to find somewhere suitable for him to live. The multidisciplinary team felt that the music therapy group could provide an environment which he might, in time, come to trust, and that the emotional focus of the work could enable him to express himself more freely.

At first, Winston appeared very motivated to take part in music therapy. He would improvise with the therapist upon a range of instruments, and suggest songs quite spontaneously, which he would then proceed to sing immediately. After about four months several new members joined the group. Winston seemed to find this very difficult and unsettling – he had become used to a small group of only two or three people. He started to sing long medleys of songs, which began to dominate the sessions and did not leave space for other people's contributions. The therapist felt under pressure to control this and frequently found herself asking him to stop singing, although she felt this was an awkward and unhelpful way of communicating with him. It was as if Winston was a child, crying out for attention, and not being satisfied. The therapist continually asked herself whether she should join in with his songs, which might be a way of involving the rest of the group, or whether she should suggest new music. Alternatively, could she find a way of drawing him into improvisation, despite his repeated refusal to play the instruments? A breakthrough came when the therapist began to improvise with Winston within the framework of his songs, which by now had become extremely familiar to her and the rest of the group. In this way she was at last able to make contact with him; it was as though the baby had stopped crying, now the mother had found out how to play with him. Gradually, from then on, Winston became far more responsive to the other group members and began to take part in music that the others offered. What now developed between him and the group was a playful exchange of songs, musical sounds, and improvisations, both melodic and harmonic. This led to Winston beginning to share some of his life experiences verbally, which in turn gave the therapist a greater understanding of his problems.

Odell-Miller also describes the changing need for structure in a group of adult clients in a mental health setting, as part of the ongoing therapeutic process. She writes:

> I have found that the best way for the group to function is to allow things to develop, and to provide musical structures at times when this seems appropriate. I provided such structure much more frequently in the first phase of the group process than in later ones, for at the beginning, the group was in the process of finding out about possibilities, of using instruments, and some members could participate only with rhythmic or harmonic support from me. During the later phases, I played less because the group was able to improvise without so much involvement from me. (1991: 424)

With Specific Clients

Other therapists have directly related the amount of musical structure needed by a client to particular emotional and psychological states. Flower describes work with adolescents in a forensic secure unit, who were considered to be a risk to society or to themselves. She writes:

> Many of the individuals on the unit had known deprivation in the area of play and creative experience. For them the spontaneity of improvisation seemed too great a demand on their inner selves. Their limited imaginative play often meant that popular tunes were endlessly and painfully recreated on the piano. (1993: 42–3)

She then goes on to describe how one teenager repeatedly played the theme tune from a television 'soap opera'.

> His use of a pre-composed melody seemed to form an important function. It offered him a safe musical starting point from which he could begin to explore the potentially unsafe world of the music therapy session. It was rather like having a musical hand to hold … In time he relinquished the use of the theme completely. It had been a springboard to greater musical creativity. (1993: 42–3)

In the next example, the progress of the music from being tightly structured to freely improvised over the period of a year connected to the specific musical skills of the group members.

The out-patient group had been meeting for three weeks in an adult mental health unit. Some of the group members were skilled musicians, who were drawn to use familiar musical structures in their playing together. The music they improvised during this period quickly turned into 'pieces' of music: one patient would create a harmonic pattern (or riff) on the keyboard, and other patients would begin to improvise around this pattern upon the melodic instruments available. Others would maintain a regular rhythm upon maracas, agogo bells and so on. The therapist also played upon percussion instruments to convey support by, for example, a simple rhythm on the temple blocks. No more than that was required for the group to feel supported in making-music. However, although much loud and energetic music was being made, it did not feel to the therapist as though any real feeling was being exchanged between people. It seemed as though they needed predictable musical formulas to make it possible for them to meet together. One year later there remained a smaller group of four committed members, and by now the music had changed. Over this period group members had begun to talk during sessions and to share difficult feelings, at one point focusing on the suicide of another patient and the distress this had caused. The therapist had also gently begun to challenge the rigidity of much of the music-making. For example, during one session, Paul, a young man of 27, had started to play a chord sequence on his guitar which he had played many times before. After listening and waiting, the therapist joined in from the piano and started to lead the music away from the tight rhythmic and harmonic progressions into music with less structure and predictability. The group talked angrily after the music had ended, feeling that she was trying to spoil Paul's music. Anger and irritation was also expressed as the therapist wondered aloud why some members were not attending on a regular basis or others were consistently arriving late. However, as these issues were addressed, it seemed to the therapist that there was now more trust between group members and herself. The music was now much more flexible, the patients were far less dependent upon tight musical structures, more confident in their musical ideas, and able to be interactive. The therapist also felt freer in response to make more music, either from the piano or other instruments, and everyone generally felt able to be more spontaneous.

The experience of attending a closed music therapy group over a period of time had enabled these changes to occur in their musical and personal relationships with each other. The clients were now able to talk about some difficult feelings they experienced in the group, such as low self-esteem and envy of other's musical contributions. This change heralded the clients being able to explore their turbulent inner worlds, both musically and verbally, and to find the sessions increasingly supportive.

Dunbar, upon identifying the significance of musical structure in her own music therapy work, carried out an investigative research project which included interviewing a sample of music therapists and analysing their thoughts and experiences. Her findings echo some of the clinical examples presented here, how 'structure is a fundamental building block of music therapy' and that 'the relationship between clinical aims, the type of group, the therapists' approach, and the structural development of the session is complex' (2001: 60–61).

Improvisation and Play

We cannot leave the topic of improvisation without a brief look at play. Winnicott (1896–1971), the paediatrician and psychoanalyst, laid a particular emphasis on the importance of play. His ideas are recognised by many music therapists (Pavlicevic, 1997: 147; Levinge, 1999) as resonating with the very specific form of 'playing' which takes place in music therapy. Winnicott's conviction that play was essential to a healthy emotional development is summed up in his words: 'It is in playing and only in playing that the individual child or adult is able to be creative and to use the whole personality, and it is only in being creative that the individual discovers the self' (1971, 1986: 63).

In his psychotherapeutic work with young children, Winnicott encouraged them to play with the toys and the other objects he had collected in his consulting room while he watched and made occasional comments or interpretations. With older children he often played the 'Squiggle' game, in which a random scrawl or 'squiggle' on a piece of paper was made into a drawing, first by the patient and then by Winnicott. The free improvised play with the toys or the improvised drawing could become the starting point for the work of the sessions, a way of making contact with his young patients and coming to understand their inner world. As a psychoanalyst working with adults, Winnicott used words, not toys, but he still maintained the idea of playing as being central to his philosophy. He wrote:

> Whatever I say about children playing really applies to adults as well, only the matter is more difficult to describe when the patient's material appears mainly in terms of verbal communication. I suggest that we must expect to find playing just as evident in the analyses of adults as is the case of our work with children. It manifests itself, for instance, in the choice of words, in the inflections of the voice, and indeed in the sense of humor. (1986: 46)

Winnicott's thinking has contributed greatly to our understanding of what possibly occurs when a client and therapist play music together and what might be happening when areas of difficulty are encountered. He also describes patients who are unable to play, that is, to be spontaneous or creative, as bringing what he terms a False Self to the analysis, speculating that the False Self begins to develop at a very early stage of the infant–mother relationship. Winnicott proposed that the 'good enough mother' can meet the demands of the infant, whereas the 'not good enough mother' is unable to do this and fails to meet what Winnicott describes as 'the infant's spontaneous gesture'. He says: 'Instead, she substitutes her own gesture which is to be given sense by the compliance of the infant. This compliance is the earliest stage of the False Self' (Winnicott, 1990: 144). He continues:

> It is an essential part of my theory that the True Self does not become a living reality except as a result of the mother's repeated success in meeting the infant's spontaneous gesture. The spontaneous gesture is the True Self in action. Only the True Self can be creative and only the True Self feels real. The existence of a False Self results in feeling unreal or a sense of futility. (1990)

The following case study (Tyler, 1998) draws together various themes that have emerged in this chapter: the continuum of structured and improvised music, the importance of play, and the relevance of theories from psychoanalytic psychotherapy to our work.

Case Study: Jennifer

Jennifer's birth was difficult, although damage was not initially suspected. Her parents described her as a miserable baby, who cried for eight months and would not be comforted. Concern grew as she failed to reach normal milestones and at thirteen months she was diagnosed as having cerebral palsy. Over the next five years Jennifer had several periods of treatment in hospital with the aim of enabling her to walk. At times she was separated from both parents, who were busy with the demands of their professional careers.

By the time she was seven, Jennifer was back at home with her parents and younger sister, now able to walk unsteadily. However, new problems were emerging. Her development was inconsistent; for example, she could read fluently but much of her speech was echolalic, repeating phrases from other people's conversations or from books. She had difficulty in forming relationships; at school she was withdrawn and ignored other children, but at home she was overbearing and imperious, particularly with her younger sister. She was primarily cared for by au pairs or nannies who kept her to a schedule of exercise and physiotherapy after school. If left to herself, however, she was described as passive, not knowing how to play, and would lie on the floor looking vacant, listening to the same cassette tapes of songs and stories over and over again, or turning the pages of an alphabet book. Because of her unrelating, stereotypical behaviour, questions were raised as to whether she was autistic.

Jennifer had weekly half-hour music therapy sessions between the ages of 7 and 11, and from the beginning she made an immediate and eager response to the situation. She showed delight in chanting nursery rhymes, imitating rhythmic patterns on the percussion instruments and organising turn-taking activities. She gave the therapist, Helen, many instructions: 'When I say 1, 2, 3, you've got to bang the drum three times,' or 'You play the high notes, I'll play the low notes,' or 'Helen, play doh, ray, me, fah, soh, lah, tee, doh!' She used phrases repetitively such as 'Today we are going to learn a new song,' or 'Now we will listen to an instrument to guess what sound it makes.' Her playing was rarely sustained and was punctuated by comments such as 'Did you hear that loud noise?' or 'What a big crash!' as though she were observing herself but not engaged on a personal level. These rigid and controlling aspects of her playing certainly were consistent with the musical responses of autistic children.

Laing, when writing about the characteristics of a False Self personality, says: 'The individual is frightened of the world, afraid that any impingement will be total, will be implosive, penetrative, fragmenting, and engulfing. He is afraid of letting anything of himself "go", of coming out of himself or of losing himself in any experience,' (1986: 83) and this described Jennifer. She demanded order, structure and predictability in the sessions and she found these in the regularity of time and place and the secure framework of greeting and goodbye songs. In the music-making, Jennifer responded to repetition, imitation, patterns and sequences, which are among the basic components of musical structure. Helen knew that Jennifer was lacking in spontaneity and creativity in her musical play, as in her general develop-ment, but she was not yet ready to play in this way. However, by attuning and responding to her immediate needs it was pos-sible to give her a new experience of what had been habitual and isolating.

As the therapy progressed, fairy-tales became a central part of each session. Week after week, month after month, the stories of Goldilocks, Little Red Riding Hood and the Three Little Pigs were recounted by Jennifer, very much as she must have heard them on her cassette tapes. The therapist's task was to illus-trate them with dramatic music and to take the part of various characters, as directed by Jennifer. Although the words of the stories were almost identical each week, Helen could alter the musical accompaniment, increasing harmonic tension and bringing in contrasts of idiom and dynamics and these changes Jennifer could accept, as long as the story structure was not altered. In the stories there was a sense of the playful-ness which is essential for the development of creativity but, despite the developing interaction and the apparent emotional expressiveness of the stories, Helen began to feel compliant, manipulated and not real as she took her part. She eventually began to experience a sense of boredom at the endless repetition of the same stories. Alvarez writing about her work with autis-tic people, says: 'The clinician treating these children may feel she is on the edge of death from boredom at witnessing a repet-itive activity for the hundredth or thousandth time, but the child never seems to get bored!' (1992: 205). Alvarez suggests that countertransference is essential here in informing the therapist that the child needs help in moving on. Helen's coun-tertransference feeling of being stuck suggested that Jennifer had become trapped in the fairy-tales. The archetypal stories had become important to Jennifer in helping her cope with early separations and painful experiences. Their predictability, however, had become part of the autistic withdrawal and was perpetuating her isolation. Therefore, she needed help to move on.

As the sessions progressed, Helen moved increasingly into areas of musical unpredictability, sometimes ignoring or playfully refusing to comply with Jennifer's demands or instructions and experimenting with slower, more serious music, with pauses and short silences. Jennifer would allow herself to be engaged, briefly, although it was hard for her to sustain and she would soon become uncomfortable, breaking in with comments and interruptions.

Out of this work, a new voice or persona emerged, this time not learned or imitated, but from an inner, unexplored part of Jennifer. The voice was alternately harsh, lyrical, playful or baby-like. In contrast to her usual vocabulary the words were very simple. 'Aah, said the lizard, I want to go home. Yes, said Helen, it's time to go. No, said the lizard, it's not time to go.'

With these words, that recurred week after week in various forms, Jennifer improvised melodies and ventured into new musical places. This was the beginning of a more spontaneous and expressive use of the sessions. Jennifer, as the lizard, could allow Helen to interact musically and emotionally with her, both of them playing and improvising in the moment. Helen connected this experience to Winnicott's use of the phrase 'spontaneous gesture' which she was able to meet so that it became creative and closer to an expression of Jennifer's True Self.

6

MUSIC THERAPY WITH CHILDREN: FOUR CASE STUDIES

When 4-year-old Sharon is brought to the music therapy clinic for a consultation session she screams and runs around, trying to get out of the door of the waiting room. Her mother cannot persuade her to walk into the music room so she brings her in the push-chair, still screaming. The room is laid out with appropriately-sized instruments, a brightly coloured drum, a shiny cymbal, bar chimes hanging from a stand, and a selection of small percussion instruments.

The music therapist, Helen, begins to play the piano, singing 'Hello Sharon' to strong, lively music that picks up the rhythm of Sharon's restless energy and the pitch of her distressed vocal sounds. Sharon's screams subside, perhaps as she hears her name sung, and recognises the intensity of her emotions being reflected in the music. She scrambles out of the push-chair, runs to the drum and begins to beat it vigorously while Helen matches her strong playing with an energetic march-like theme. Sharon soon throws the stick on the floor as her attention is caught by the shimmering bar chimes on the other side of the room. She runs over to them, rippling them with her fingers, and the music from the piano becomes soft, swirling and dreamy. Sharon can't stay with this quiet mood for long and runs back to the drum. This time, when Helen joins her with the march-like theme, Sharon glances at her briefly, as though recognising that the music has a connection with what she is doing. She pauses in her beating, and seems to notice that Helen stops playing too. She repeats this, checking each time to see if Helen is imitating her. For the next 15 minutes Sharon continues to alternate between the drum and the chimes, showing an increasing awareness of the relationship between her actions and the music Helen is playing. Her fleeting moments of eye contact with Helen and her smiles towards her mother, who is watching, seem to indicate recognition of this new experience.

Sharon has a diagnosis of autistic spectrum disorder. This condition is characterised by difficulties in three principal areas: communication, social interaction and imaginative play (Wing and Gould, 1979: 11–29). She does not speak and shows little interest in people or things around her. She has eating problems, refusing almost everything except crisps, and is hyperactive, constantly on the move. She is only calm and focused when watching videos or television programmes, although her parents worry that this is becoming obsessional.

In speaking with her mother, Helen found out that the 20-minute consultation session had been an unusually long time for Sharon to sustain a shared activity with another person, and that it was rare for her to show such signs of awareness, pleasure and interaction.

This first encounter between Helen and Sharon demonstrates one way in which a music therapist might make contact with a young client in a first session. The therapist listens attentively to the pitch, the timbre and the intensity of the sounds the child makes in vocalising, crying or screaming. She observes the tempo and rhythm of the child's breathing and gestures. She uses these observations to form the beginnings of a musical language with which to make a connection, a language which can be expressive without words. As we saw in Chapter 1, this way of working relates to the earliest communication between parent and infant. Child psychologists have frequently used words from musical terminology, such as phrasing, timing, tuning and dynamics, to describe parent–infant interactions, while many of the skills intuitively used by parents to engage their babies are part of the music therapist's technique. Helen, in seeking to make an initial contact with Sharon, was listening, and attuning then imitating, reflecting and mirroring. Although music was the medium used by Helen, the therapeutic goals which gradually emerged were not specifically musical, but related to Sharon's whole personality and the difficulties she was experiencing in all areas of her life.

Pavlicevic warns the music therapist against limiting expectations of the child through seeing them only in terms of their pathology or their chronological age and urges a 'synchronous' view which accepts the whole child. Describing a child with autism, she writes:

I hear the quality of the whole child in the therapist's music: the shifts, the weight, the contours, colour and motion of how she is. Through my music therapist's listening skills, I have an essential sense of this child: one that seems to cut across her developmental stage, her disorder and limitations ... and that offers me a synthesis of all that she is, in the moment of music. I hear and experience 'The Child in Health and Time'. (2001: 14)

After the consultation session, Sharon was offered ongoing music therapy to help her in the areas of communication, self-expression and play. As trust developed in the course of the ongoing therapy, the more complex interactions of turn-taking and sharing became a focus of the sessions. Sharon's difficult emotional states – her demands, screams and tantrums – were also met in the music. As we have already seen in Chapter 2, a vital part of therapy is to work with the resistive reaction as well as with participation.

The pioneers of music therapy in the UK, Alvin and Nordoff and Robbins, worked extensively with children in special education establishments and in hospitals. Their descriptions of work in the 1960s and 70s make it clear that they, too, had goals that extended beyond the musical activities which they were offering to meet the whole child. Alvin writes:

The ideal which has guided me throughout the work is a conviction, based on fact, that music should be a creative experience and that it should help to discover or exploit to the full any ability the child may possess in various fields, not necessarily in music ... The child's individual response to music very often reveals a non-musical need and shows how he [or she] can be reached and helped. (1978: 3–4)

Similarly, Nordoff and Robbins considered that their work had aims which were neither purely musical nor educational. They state that:

It is the music therapists' role to supplement the educational and class-room activities of the teacher with a programme aimed at providing special experiences that have central psychological significance for the children, and which can be therapeutic for their whole development. The strengthening of ego-function, the liberation from emotional restriction and the alleviation of behavioural problems, all make for happier, more fulfilled children who can participate more fully in their school life and derive greater benefit from it. (1992: 139)

The children who received music therapy in the early days of the profession were very often in institutions, either long-stay hospitals or residential homes. Children with severe physical disabilities or illnesses were deemed to be 'ineducable' in the terminology of the day and were therefore not eligible to attend school. Lack of support and help for their parents meant that it was inevitable that many would spend most of their lives in hospitals or institutions. Since those days, however, the lives of children with disabilities have been affected profoundly by changes in legislation, health and education policy and by advances in medicine. 1970 was a watershed in expanding the opportunities available, through the Education (Handicapped Children) Act 1970, which for the first time gave a statutory entitlement to education for all children. The Warnock Report (Committee of Enquiry into the Education of Handicapped Children and Young People, 1978) was the first to recommend the inclusion or integration of children with special needs into mainstream education and this was subsequently enshrined in the 1981 Education Act. In healthcare, too, there have been enormous advances and most long-stay children's hospitals have now closed to be replaced by smaller, specialised units. Improved surgical and medical techniques have led to many more premature babies surviving, although some may be severely brain-damaged. In the same way, children with life-threatening or life-limiting conditions can now have a longer life-expectancy and with improved quality of life, though they may need long-term medical care. Thus the range of children referred to music therapy has broadened considerably since the days of the pioneers. While music therapists still treat those with diagnoses of cerebral palsy, autism and Downs Syndrome and are active within hospitals and special education, a more complex pattern of work is now developing. Music therapy is currently used:

- as a diagnostic tool for assessing communication disorder and autism (Wigram, 1999);
- as part of multi-disciplinary early intervention programmes for mothers and their young children who have developmental disabilities (Oldfield and Bunce, 2001);
- with children hospitalised for cancer or other invasive medical treatments (Pavlicevic, 1999);
- in hospice work with terminally ill children, including therapy for the whole family, not just the patient (Ibberson, 1996);
- with adolescent patients with eating disorders, which are now accepted as being psychological illnesses (Robarts, 1994);
- as an intervention for children who have been sexually abused or who are considered to be at risk from abuse of any sort (Rogers, 1992, 1993); and

- post-traumatic stress work with children who are suffering psychological effects from accident, disaster, war or family tragedy (Sutton, 2002).

As well as children who are identified as having particular needs or circumstances requiring therapy, referrals of a less specific nature are also made. For example, the SENCO (Special Educational Needs Coordinator) of a mainstream primary school recently referred three children to a music therapy clinic from a long waiting list. One was a 9-year-old boy whose behaviour and academic progress had deteriorated after his father's sudden death. The second was an 11-year-old girl who had started playing truant from school but had not managed to tell anyone what was worrying her, and the third was the child of a refugee family, who was described as being withdrawn and having very low self-esteem. None of these children had a formal diagnosis of Special Educational Needs, but they were all struggling with school, social relations and with talking about their problems. Music therapy is now recognised as having a contribution to make in helping troubled children, whether their issues are physical, emotional, behavioural, cognitive or a complex combination of all of them.

To illustrate some of the ways in which a music therapist might approach work with children, we will now focus upon some clinical examples, beginning with a look at group work, followed by two more detailed individual case studies.

Group Music Therapy for Children

Children, even more than adults, spend most of their waking lives in groups, first at home in the family, then at school and frequently in after-school or weekend group activities. Music in particular draws children together, whether through organised singing and playing in choirs, orchestras and bands, or in activities where music is significant such as dancing, from ballet to pop. As Hargreaves and North write, 'Music has many different functions in human life, nearly all of them social' (1997: 1).

Music therapy, too, takes place in groups in a variety of different settings. These include mainstream or special schools at nursery, primary or secondary levels and also specialised units for children with specific needs such as autism, speech and language difficulties, behavioural or psychiatric problems. Group music therapy uses music as the main medium through which the needs of both the individual child and the group are met by offering opportunities for child–adult and child–child interaction. In order to achieve this it is necessary for the groups to be small, for example, four children, in contrast to a class music lesson where every child would be present.

Vignette: Nursery Group

The group consists of three children with cerebral palsy, Mark and Mary, (4 years old) and Jamie (3½) who are in the nursery class of a school for children with physical disabilities. They all have problems with walking, fine motor control and speech, while Jamie has additional learning difficulties. They have some understanding of language but are in the early stages of verbal communication, using single words. They have not passed through the usual stages of crawling, toddling, babbling and exploring the world through play and experimentation and each is to some extent isolated by his or her pathology. The amount of physical care on which the children are dependent means that they are far more used to being with adults than with their peers.

Although there is plenty of day-to-day musical activity in the classroom, particularly singing games and action songs, the concentrated focus of the therapy session is seen by school staff as giving a unique contribution to the children's development. It gives an opportunity for self-expression and creativity as well as pleasure and a sense of achievement. In addition to these observable benefits of participating in the session, the music therapist, Robin, hopes to meet the children's emotional needs through the different experiences which are offered. This means acknowledging feelings of frustration, impatience, anger, rivalry, discomfort or anxiety, and finding ways of expressing them within the music. This acceptance of 'negative' or difficult feelings as material to be worked with musically is a vital part of the music therapy process, and differentiates it from other forms of music-making.

The Session

The session takes place in a corner of the nursery classroom, where there is a piano and a selection of percussion instruments. Robin, who visits the school once a week, is assisted by Christine, the nursery nurse who works in the class. First, Robin sings a greeting song to each child, leaving a space for their responses, and encouraging them to reach out to touch his guitar as he plays. Mary is instantly aware and engaged while Mark seems distracted, looking around the room. Jamie, who has only just started school, is shy and reluctant to participate, hiding his face in his hands. Robin allows each child to respond in their own way and in their own time, so instead of urging Jamie to join in, he improvises a peek-a-boo song for him, which in turn interests Mark who wants to call out 'Boo!' to Jamie.

After this Robin moves to the piano as the children take turns to play a large tambourine, held for them by Christine. Mary plays with big, random and uncontrolled arm movements which Robin supports with dramatic chords on the piano, timed to coincide with her hand making contact with the tambourine. Gradually, her beating becomes more controlled, and she finds a regular pulse so that she and Robin are playing in time together. When it is Jamie's turn, he won't play, but leans across the tambourine rocking. Robin moves into a gentle rocking tempo singing that 'Jamie is rowing his boat on the tambourine'. This acknowledges Jamie's reluctance to play, while making a musical connection with his spontaneous rocking movements. Mark wants to kick the tambourine and Robin hears him sing the opening of the theme music of a popular football programme, *Match of the Day*. This leads to everyone wanting to 'score a goal' by kicking the tambourine while Robin improvises the song on the piano. Although none of the children can walk independently they are all spontaneously motivated to move their legs and feet to kick, and even Jamie copies the others to have a turn. Here, the flow between a pre-composed song and improvisation is seamless, one moving into the other as the situation requires.

Next, each child has a chance to choose an instrument to improvise freely while Robin plays the piano. Mary chooses the bar chimes which she plays with large sweeping movements, and Robin accompanies with impressionistic rippling music, reminiscent of Debussy's *En Bateau*. Mary's movements follow the rise and fall of the music and she shows a clear sense of phrasing and structure. She puts tremendous energy and concentration into her playing, and it seems to be an emotionally satisfying experience for her. Mark is restless while she plays, finding it hard to wait for his turn while another child is the centre of attention. He chooses the drum and beats strongly but erratically, using two sticks with alternate hands, to march-like music. His left side is weak, and he usually avoids using his left hand, but here he is motivated to put great effort into his playing and struggles to stabilise his beating into a satisfying even tempo. When he achieves it and he and Robin are 'marching' along together, a huge smile lights up his face. Jamie chooses bells, which he shakes while Robin sings *Ding, dong bell*. The other children join in vocally, approximating the sounds of 'ding dong', and they are all given bells to shake as a 'ding dong' song develops.

Finally Christine selects small instruments for the children to blow while Robin improvises a lilting waltz melody. The older two have reed horns, pitched a 4th apart, while Jamie, who has difficulty in focusing his breath, has the top of a recorder which makes a sound more easily. At first the children blow at random, absorbed in their own activity. This corresponds to the stage of child development in which young children play side by side, in parallel play, seemingly unaware of each other. As they start listening to each other and the piano, they begin to co-ordinate their sounds and there is more awareness of themselves, their peers and how each part fits into the music. The fact that they are using their lips, tongue and breathing in a controlled blowing motion is noted by Christine as being helpful to their speech development, but to the children it is 'playing', both musically and in being playful. The 'musical conversations' which develop between the children and Robin are more fluent than any they could manage in words.

Now a goodbye song is sung with the guitar, again with a space for each child to respond. Like the greeting song, this is repeated week after week, creating a familiar and consistent framework, letting the children know what is happening, and setting the time boundaries for the session. Their voices are more focused and confident than at the beginning of the session. Mark and Mary wave and sing 'bye' while Jamie gives Robin direct eye contact as his name is sung. Christine comments that the children all seem more alert than before the music therapy session, and that Jamie seems to be settling into the group.

This is a glimpse of only one session with a particular group of children and therefore does not cover the whole range of different group experiences which can be offered. However, it reveals some of the music therapist's techniques as he creates musical situations to engage the children, to build on their strengths and work with their areas of need.

Individual Music Therapy

The two children who will be described in individual therapy are in many ways very different. Tom will never develop speech and will need care and support for the rest of his life, while Carl has the potential to live an independent and productive life. Both, however, had developmental, emotional and psychological needs which had not been met in their early lives and which could be explored through the medium of music therapy.

Case Study: Tom

Tom was born with Downs Syndrome and severe learning disabilities and, at 5-years-old, was also diagnosed with autistic spectrum disorder. As a baby he was deprived of normal care as his mother had severe mental health problems for which she was reluctant to seek help. When Tom was 2-years-old, concerns expressed by neighbours led to social workers finding him lying neglected in a cot, surrounded by litter which his mother had hoarded obsessively. He had been fed only with a bottle and had developed many self-stimulating behaviours, such as rocking, eye-poking, head-banging and sucking his clothes. Similar characteristics have been observed in children who have been institutionalised from an early age and deprived of the opportunity for bonding with a mother or parental figure.

Tom was taken into care and attempts were made to help his mother, but she disappeared without trace. Tom was subsequently fostered and, at 5-years-old, adopted by his foster parents. At that time he did not know how to relate to people, made no eye contact and had no speech. He was physically active, running up and down, twirling round and round or rocking repetitively and, significantly, he did not know how to play. As mentioned in Chapter 5, child specialists agree that playing is essential for a child's healthy emotional growth (Winnicott, 1986: 48), and that the lack of ability to play spontaneously is one of the major impairments of autism. An autistic child replaces creative or imaginative play with stereotyped and repetitive activities, and uses toys or other objects to twiddle, twirl or suck rather than recognising the purpose for which they were intended. For example, a child might carry a toy car around with him and spin the wheels, instead of playing with it imaginatively. The car could then be described as an 'autistic object', a concept first described by Tustin (1972) which hinders play and interaction.

When he was six, Tom began to attend a special school part-time, but was not able to cope even with the nursery class, so unused was he to being with or relating to other people. However, he always responded to music in the classroom, twirling round in circles, or sitting with his ear resting against the loud speaker. This gave his adoptive mother the idea of trying music therapy as a way of breaking through his isolation.

Tom's First Music Therapy Session

To watch Tom at 6-years-old, in his first session, was to see a child apparently having fun, laughing and vocalising as he beat a stick on a large shiny cymbal. He was obviously motivated and excited as he went round and round in circles, caught up in the sounds he was making, with his face close to the vibrating surface of the instrument. The music was giving him a new experience of his habitual twirling activity without taking him away from his familiar sensory world.

At first he was apparently unaware of Helen's presence at the piano, as she joined his tempo of beating and matched his vocal sounds, hoping to make a connection. However, as the session progressed, he began to make brief pauses in his continuous playing and to give fleeting glances in the direction of the piano, as though he was aware that there was someone alongside him who was not intruding directly on him. Helen was here using the techniques described earlier, similar to those used when a mother, listening and attending to her baby, matches and imitates the sounds that the baby makes. At the end of the session, when it was time to leave, Tom threw himself to the floor and refused to move, eventually having to be carried from the room.

As the sessions continued it became clear that when Tom was left to play the instruments freely, whether the drum, piano or cymbal, he withdrew into an isolated but comfortable world of sound and movement. Helen wondered if it felt like the familiar world of the cot in which he had spent his early years, stimulating himself with his own sounds and sensations. Using a musical metaphor, the child psychotherapist, Ann Alvarez, describes the way in which an autistic child can get stuck in repetitive or ritualistic activities:

> When you are interacting with living human objects, they are not perfect mirrors; they talk back, move, surprise; by definition you cannot easily get stuck. Autistic objects are dead ends, and while the child's original motive for turning to the object may gradually fade, the melodyless [sic] behaviour lingers on. (Alvarez and Reid, 1999: 73)

As we have seen, Tom used objects, such as the musical instruments, in a repetitive way, but in music therapy something was different.

The musical instruments could 'talk back', both through their acoustic properties and through Helen's response in reflecting Tom's sounds back to him and enhancing them with her own music. In this way Tom and Helen could create meaning and a melody together. It continued to be difficult for Tom to leave the room at the end of the session and he would cry as though devastated at the loss of the therapy. This situation also arose at home and school at times of transition; it was as though Tom had no sense of the permanency of people or places. For this reason it was important to prepare for the ending of each session in good time, and to sing the same good-bye song every week. This could be compared to the bed-time ritual where the reassuring story, song and words prepare the young child for the nightly separation and serve as a reminder that mother will still be there in the morning.

Tom's Continuing Therapy
After the initial exploratory sessions, Helen wrote a report for Tom's parents and teachers, outlining the aims which she saw emerging. These were to help Tom to develop listening skills, playfulness, turn-taking and sharing. Tom needed to be shown how to take turns in playing a drum or how to play peek-a-boo behind the piano. Concepts like 'up and down' (when Helen playfully moved a tambourine up and down for Tom to play), 'round and round and stop' (dancing round in a circle together then stopping) or 'ready, steady, crash!' (anticipating a cymbal crash) all helped Tom to become aware of himself in relation to Helen. It also gave him an experience of the playful communication which develops naturally between a mother and her baby. Stern speaks of 'affect attunement' in describing the way a mother responds spontaneously to her baby's communication (Stern, 1985). If she is over-stimulating, the baby may be overwhelmed and become upset, while an emotionally flat response can cause the baby to withdraw from the interaction.

By the sixth month of therapy, Tom was able to leave his habitual repetitive and stereotyped behaviour patterns for short periods and join Helen in a musical activity. Each session also allowed Tom the freedom to explore a range of instruments and he became particularly interested in strumming a small lyre, tuned to a pentatonic scale. He allowed Helen to sit close to him on the floor while he played, so that she could intervene to take a turn and sing softly about what he was doing.

By the end of the first year of therapy it was possible to engage Tom in playing a musical game, based on a loose rondo structure and using his favourite instrument, the cymbal. His free energetic playing on the cymbal to improvised music led back each time to a musical refrain with the words 'Crash goes the cymbal NOW!'. This gave Tom a verbal cue when to play the cymbal crash, which was accompanied by a dramatic chord on the piano. His anticipation of the word 'NOW' showed that he had remembered and internalised the structure of the song. His playing on the cymbal, which had seemed like repetitive autistic behaviour in earlier sessions, had become part of a creative experience, shared with Helen. He showed increasing self-control and self-awareness as he responded to the familiar song, and his playful enjoyment was apparent from his squeals of laughter.

Meanwhile, Tom was settling into the pattern of school life, taking more notice of the people around him, and generally becoming more sociable and communicative. Leaving the room at the end of a session became manageable, as though Tom had realised that 'goodbye' was not forever. After two years of therapy, Tom was ready to attend school full-time, and was enjoying many activities including riding and swimming, and was more able to take part in school group activities. It was decided between the therapist, teacher and parents that it was the right time to finish his music therapy, although it was impossible to know how much Tom understood of the process.

In his music therapy sessions Tom had initially revealed his innate responsiveness to the elements of music, in particular the sensory properties of vibration, rhythm and movement. The element that was lacking from his experience was that of a relationship, so that music was an isolating rather than a social or shared phenomenon. Through working initially with his habitual responses, Helen was able to lead him into play and eventually enable Tom to discover an awareness of himself and a sense of autonomy.

Case Study: Carl

The second case study is of Carl, a boy of 10, who attended a mainstream primary school. Carl lived alone with his mother and had only occasional contact with his father. His mother described Carl's birth as 'an accident', and subsequently went on to blame the hospital where he was born for his behavioural problems, which she claimed were a result of various allergies he had developed in childhood. She had a great fear of infections, and was constantly cleaning her house and 'scrubbing' her son.

> *Carl had exhibited disturbed behaviour from nursery school onwards where he had become known as disruptive and aggressive. His mother saw him as 'picked on' by children and teachers and also said that 'he didn't know his own strength, so he sometimes hurt people.' He had been referred to child guidance from the school and had received psychotherapy for 14 months. His diagnosis from a paediatrician stated that he was behaviourally immature, in the low average cognitive range, with poor organisation and concentration and some features of developmental dispraxia and dyslexia.*

Knowing a little of Carl's history and of his aggressive behaviour, the therapist, Helen, decided to work with a male co-therapist, Mark, who could match Carl's physical strength if necessary but could also help to provide a model of positive parenting.

From the beginning it was clear that Carl was in great need of emotional release as he hammered the instruments and tore round the room. He shouted a barrage of instructions at the therapists as he acted out stories based on the superhero figures from cartoons, such as *Batman, Superman* and *Power Rangers*. He always wanted to take the role of the bad character and to fight Mark, while Helen was to provide suitably dramatic background music. It was very difficult to hold the boundaries – Mark would use the tambourine as a shield while Carl hit it but it was clear that he wanted a real fight. In the following transcription of an extract from the first session Helen is at the piano, accompanying Carl's actions and repeating his words, sometimes in song. Carl, very excited, is shouting, his voice occasionally taking on a musical inflection.

EXTRACT 1

Carl: [shouting] I'm a really nasty knight, the power-fullest! [*fighting gestures and noises to Mark*] You die!

Mark: [falls down] Aaaargh!

Carl: [dramatically] Ha ha ha ha! Fear not, I'll always live, no dead can fight me. Ha ha ha ha! Anyway, the wicked witch made me, so no-one can win me. She gave me magical powers and a sword that can fling any power back. Ha ha ha!

Helen: [singing] Here's the wicked witch with magic power ...

Carl: [interrupting] I'm not the wicked witch. *She* gave me the magic power and I'm a really nasty knight. I'm not a wicked witch, I'm the really nasty knight and I'm a hunter. I've got the *most* magical powers – she made me.

Helen: She made you?

Carl: No, she didn't.

Helen: She gave you her magic power?

Carl: I and my really magical powers and she's a wicked witch, and she tells me what to do.

Immediately we enter the world of mythology and make-believe, which links ancient folk stories through fairy-tales to the modern-day boy magician, Harry Potter (Rowling: 1997). The nasty knight, the wicked witch, the hunter and their magical powers are all universal concepts, or archetypes. The psychoanalyst Kalsched, paraphrasing Jung, said that 'mythology is where the psyche was before psychology made it an object of scientific investigation (1996: 6). Kalsched, in describing his work with adult patients, considers that their dreams, fantasy and mythology hold the key to discovering the inner traumas they may have suffered in childhood. He defines trauma in a broad sense as meaning 'any experience which causes the child unbearable psychic pain or anxiety' ranging from 'shattering experiences of child abuse' to 'unmet dependency needs' (1996: 1). Carl, from his first session, displayed acute anxiety under the guise of omnipotent self-sufficiency and toughness.

To the collection of archetypal figures Carl brought into the first session, a new one soon appeared – that of the Riddler. This character occurs in the *Batman* stories which Carl frequently enacted. The Riddler can change shape, take different disguises and play tricks on innocent people. The origins of this character are ancient, an example being the serpent in the Garden of Eden. Jung identified this figure as 'The Trickster' and describes it as carrying both sides of a split in the psyche (Jung, 1972: 133–52). It can also be linked with the concept of the mask and with Winnicott's concept of the True and False Self (Tyler, 1998).

In the following extract taken from the third month of therapy, Carl pretends to be the powerful Lord Zed who, disguised as a baby, is waiting to attack Mark. Acting the part of a crying baby allows Carl to express some of his own 'needy baby' feelings in a way which does not expose his true vulnerability. Here Carl's omnipotent persona is a mask which is necessary to protect him from the painful reality of being the baby, unwanted by his father and his mother.

From the piano Helen responds musically to his crying sounds and acknowledges his pain, while Mark takes an active part in the drama. Carl's ambivalence in revealing his neediness is shown as he pleads with Mark to pick him up and then attacks him physically. All this is contained within a musical framework based on the whole tone scale, which is itself an ambiguous form of musical expression, constructed out of three white notes, C-D-E followed by three black notes F#-G#-A#.

EXTRACT 2

Carl: [crawls under the piano, making 'baby noises'] Goo goo, goo goo, gaa gaa gaa.

Helen: [sings] Goo goo gaa gaa.

Carl: [to Mark] You come along … (more baby noises) I'm dressed up like a baby, right, you have to come along …

Mark: It's a baby!
[Carl makes baby crying noises which are increasingly intense, falling into the tonality of the music Helen is playing.]

Helen: [sings] I can hear a baby crying.

Carl: Pretend Lord Zed came out, I was dressed up like a baby – yeah, I was in disguise.

Mark: It's a baby!

Carl: I come out, you have to be frightened. You have to push me along … lift me up, you have to try to lift me up, I'm a baby. Lord Zed was there – pick me up, go on, pick me up!
[Jumps out from under the piano and attacks Mark]

Mark: Oh no, another trick!

Carl: Two tricks, never mind, I said.

The theme of evil overcoming good was predominant in the first year of work, whether it was through the superheroes of cartoons or the muggers and murderers of *Crime Watch*, a television programme which Carl often acted out. This seems to illustrate Kalsched's assertion that in response to trauma the self appears as radical opposites, good/bad, love/hate, healing/destruction.

Meanwhile, it seemed that things were not good at school. Carl was getting further behind his peers academically and was extremely unpopular with staff and pupils. His mother was constantly going to the school to complain about discrimination against him, but she seemed to trust the music therapists enough to bring Carl regularly for his sessions.

The sessions were hard physical and emotional work for the therapists, but there were some hopeful signs. For example, Carl found the end of each session increasingly difficult, often lying on the floor, pretending to be injured or dead, and so beginning to recognise his dependency on the therapists. Mark and Helen could at these times express feelings of sadness, while he would listen, with satisfaction, joining in with moans or cries. This acknowledged his sense of loss for what he had perhaps never known, and allowed him to grieve for it. Carl also began to sing more in the sessions, often arias with thoughtful and moving words, for example, 'Time passes, time goes on and on, I wish I could stop the time.' On one occasion he altered the hands on the clock, trying to gain some extra session time. Carl, a boy who could read only with difficulty and did not have the concentration to write stories, could be creative, expressive and poetic within the safely-contained musical environment of the sessions.

One of Carl's arias, 17 months into the therapy, had a particular significance in that he was able for the first time to link the fantasy world of wizards and witches with his own fantasies, desires and anxieties. Carl was lying on the floor as he half-sung and half-spoke the words, supported by a 'blues' sequence played on the piano which provided stability and containment with its clear structure and repetition.

EXTRACT 3

Carl: Oh, if Mark could just be my friend! Oh, if Mark …
I–I the power – I don't know, I'm not powerful,
I'm not wicked, it's just this witch, the wizard, has done something bad to me.
I know I'm not a wizard, but I've learned magic from someone.
I was only a boy, I never was a wizard, I was just an ordinary boy.
And my Dad gave me the magic, and Mum so I could become a good wizard.

They always knew I was good, they always knew I never meant things,
But it was just this witch who put powder in my head.
I try to vanish this bad witch on me when my power breaks.

> My power's not strong, it's a little bit of wood.
> I'm sorry, oh my God, so sorry I've never had good friends.

Shortly after this a new character, 'The Bully', appeared in the sessions as Carl explored his immediate problems at school. The fantasy element, while still present, was mediated by more of a sense of reality. Carl participated vigorously in singing a song which Helen improvised, 'Everyone's afraid of the Bully, 'cause he's big and strong.' Alongside this realism was a wish for something better, which Carl expressed in an unselfconscious attempt to fly by running very fast and jumping. He was able to let go of his omnipotence and accept that he wasn't Superman flying gracefully through the sky, but a boy coming down to earth with a bump.

Soon after this Carl's music therapy came to a sudden end with his move to a new school. Regrettably, his mother took him away without allowing a session to say goodbye and would not enter into any discussion about it. The therapists wrote to Carl, but did not hear from him or see him again and they were left with anger at 'the witch' who had 'vanished' him away, a sense of loss, and feelings of having been 'not good enough' parents who failed to protect him. However, despite all, Helen and Mark felt that in the course of therapy Carl had developed inner resources and some insight into his problems, so perhaps after all, he would be able to access his 'magical powers' to help him cope with life.

Despite the differences between Sharon, Mark, Mary, Jamie, Tom and Carl, the music therapist uses similar principles when working with them all. The improvised music expresses something of the essence of each child, so that their strengths and needs are sounded in the therapy room. This is a starting point from which to develop a relationship which can address both feeling states and developmental needs. As Trevarthen and Malloch express it:

> Music is much more than just 'non-verbal' or 'pre-verbal', and its use in therapy is based in the life-long human trait of creating companionship with another by structuring expressive time together... Therapy by 'conversational improvisation' of music is an art and clinical technique that directly addresses human intersubjective feelings and expressions in time. (2000: 14)

7

IT CAN BE A ROUGH
VOYAGE ... (WORKING
THROUGH SETBACKS)

Throughout this book we have discussed how music therapists develop ways to engage and interact with their clients through music, in order to fulfil therapeutic goals. However, clients who come to music therapy do not always play music, either because they cannot or because they do not want to. This can cause much anxiety for the new or experienced music therapist alike: surely music therapy is about playing music? Can the music therapy still help, even if clients do not play music, or is it inappropriate to continue offering them sessions? In this chapter we will examine some issues which arise when clients:

- are unable to or do not wish to use the instruments;
- are inhibited by anxiety about musical skill; or
- use instruments symbolically instead of playing them.

We will also look at the function of talking in music therapy, ranging from the minimal functional use of words, to situations in which clients choose to talk, rather than to play music.

Clients Who are Unable to Play

Mike

Mike crouches in the corner of the music room. His hands cover his face – he has a finger up each nostril and fingers in his ears. His eyes are screwed tightly shut. It is as though he is determined that nothing is going to get inside him, or escape from him. The music therapist, Helen, sitting in the middle of the room, plays a single note on a chime bar and sings his name. There is no visible or audible response. After a while, Helen moves to sit nearer to Mike, but as she approaches him, he shouts out and, springing to his feet, takes up a position in the opposite corner, as far away from Helen as possible. He begins to pace up and down the room, anxiously. Helen, avoiding looking at Mike or making eye contact with him, improvises some warm, steady music on the piano in time with his footsteps, and gradually Mike becomes calmer. He moves back across the room and comes to stand by the piano, behind Helen. He looks up at the ceiling, his hands clasped in front of his body. His posture now seems more relaxed as though at this point, halfway through the session, he is more open to receive the music. He continues to reject any direct approach, and consistently refuses to touch the instruments which Helen offers to him.

Mike was a tall, middle-aged man, born in London, who had spent most of his life in institutions. A major epileptic fit at 2-years-old had caused serious brain damage and led to him being placed in a residential hospital for children. As a young adult he was moved to a large Victorian psychiatric hospital in the countryside which was to be his home for 20 years. Mike was a solitary person, who had no speech and showed very little interest in communicating with people around him. He would spend long periods on his own, curled up or rocking, but he also liked walking, and would cover great distances around the extensive hospital grounds. When Mike was 40, a process began of moving the residents out of the hospital, as plans were being made for it to close down. People were, wherever possible, to be resettled near their place of origin, so Mike was moved back to London, to a tall terraced house in a busy street. Three other former hospital residents shared the house, supported by a team of social care workers, and together they attended a day centre. It soon became apparent that Mike found the lack of personal space in his new life, and in particular living in close proximity to other people, very distressing. On several occasions he managed to get out of the day centre and was found wandering in a park, some miles away. He found it very hard when the group in his house sat down together for a meal or to watch television, and if other people made a noise, he would begin to make howling sounds, sometimes hitting out or grabbing them.

Mike was referred to music therapy in the hope that it could address his feelings about having moved from his familiar home to the city, a decision over which he had no control. The music therapist, Helen, also hoped that, through music, she would be able to work with the difficulty he had in forming relationships, in spite of the fact that initially he did all that he could to shut himself off from her. Helen kept the room free from clutter so that there was plenty of space for Mike to walk around and to move away from her and the source of the music when he needed to. She would improvise, using the piano, the other instruments and her voice, but would also sometimes sit in silence, so that there was space and freedom from sound in the room. Over time, even though Mike maintained his physical distance from Helen, the music began to act as a bridge between them. Throughout the two-year period over which he attended music therapy, Mike did not voluntarily play a single note on any of the instruments. However, his posture and his facial expression became increasingly open, and he became able to look at Helen and tolerate her looking at him. The music became a shared creation with Mike's contribution being his listening, his attentiveness and his silence. Through the music therapy Mike was increasingly able to:

- tolerate being in an enclosed space with another person;
- react without panic at being approached; and
- tolerate, and eventually respond to, sounds made by another person.

Clare

Like Mike, 5-year-old Clare did not willingly reach out to touch or play any of the instruments she was offered in her group music therapy sessions. In contrast to him, though, she seemed to enjoy the sound of loud, lively music and was particularly attracted by bright, shiny instruments. If chimes, bells or a tambourine were played near her, she would track their movement with her eyes, squealing with delight and kicking her legs. She also seemed to enjoy the therapist singing to her, joining in with extended and expressive vocalisations.

Clare was generally smiling and sociable, except on days when she was affected by epileptic seizures which resulted from

Rett's Syndrome, the genetic condition from which she suffered. The features of Rett's syndrome, which generally become apparent at about 18 months, include the loss of many of the cognitive and motor skills previously learned and a regression to a very early stage of development. The hand movements of people with Rett's syndrome become repetitive and stereotyped, either clapping or clasping the hands together, or constantly putting them into the mouth. When Clare began music therapy she was very reluctant to play with the instruments as she was not able to hold or reach out for objects. Instead she would suck her fingers or wrap them in her clothing, making it clear that she did not want her hands to be touched. She had a very short attention span, and could become very tense, holding her breath, if put under any pressure.

These characteristics, combined with Clare's inability to access the instruments, might make Clare seem an unlikely referral for music therapy. Her teacher, however, was very keen for her to join a small group with three other children. So what benefits could Clare gain from her music therapy sessions? Her school report, written by the music therapist at the end of the year, listed the following areas:

- improvised music and songs could match her lively moods or express her feelings when she was upset or subdued;
- music enabled Clare to communicate, extending her vocal range and encouraging interaction with the therapist;
- music stimulated her awareness of her body movements, for example, kicking a tambourine or swinging her arms to music with the therapist's assistance;
- Clare became more aware of her peers, through watching them playing; and
- she enjoyed the sessions and therefore became physically relaxed. This enabled her to accept the sensation of some of the instruments touching her hands.

The Use of Words by the Therapist

Most therapists will use a basic minimum of words to facilitate the start, continuation or ending of a therapy session. These words might include:

- greeting the client and putting them at ease;
- asking 'Which instrument would you like to play?' or 'Do you want to change instrument?';
- setting time boundaries such as 'It's almost time to finish now';
- saying goodbye, and confirming the next session.

These words, however, may serve more than the purely functional purpose of conveying information and the practical details of the session, as we shall see in the following case example.

The setting was an acute in-patient ward in a mental health unit where an open music therapy session was provided on a weekly basis. On this occasion five young men attended the group, Royston, Michael, Juan, Andy and Bruce. They were all quite seriously ill, some suffering from psychotic delusions. The music therapist, Rachel, was assisted by Justin, a nurse, who was also a musician. Without needing verbal prompting, the clients immediately chose instruments and started to play loud, chaotic music. Nobody seemed to be listening to anybody else and it was as though they were all competing to be heard. Royston was playing the guitar, strumming the open strings as loudly as possible; Michael was playing a fast rhythmic pattern on the conga drums; Bruce was playing another drum with a stick, its sound resonating at great volume. Andy was playing the xylophone, sweeping his two sticks backwards and forwards across the keys in a rather desultory way, while Juan was playing a rapid rhythm on the agogo bells with a wooden stick, its sound alone almost drowning the group. Rachel began by playing a drum, but could not hear herself and so moved to the piano. She decided that her role in the middle of all the sounds was to listen to everybody and, amidst all the chaos, to resist the temptation to try to take control. The music continued for 10 long minutes. Then, the clients all stopped quite spontaneously and suddenly fell very quiet. Both Rachel and Justin made some comments about how the music had sounded to them. They quickly realised, though, that everything had been said in the music and the clients appeared to have nothing to add verbally. Rachel then made the suggestion, 'Shall we all change instruments?' The non-verbal response of the group seemed to indicate the wish to do this, as they all stood up eagerly and moved to different instruments. The music that followed was less frenzied, and people began to be able to listen, and to respond to each other a little.

This example illustrates a scenario where only a minimal use of words was necessary. Words were needed simply to structure the session and to move it forward into a new phase. Verbal interaction and reflection were not comfortable or meaningful ways for these clients to communicate, so that not being required to speak, together with the opportunity to express themselves through music, was more beneficial.

Words as Part of the Music

Another possibility is that the client begins to talk during the music. In Chapter 5 we presented an understanding of how all sounds in the therapy session might be heard as music and this includes the spoken word. This could mean that on some occasions the therapist continues to play whilst the client talks. On the other hand, sometimes it feels more appropriate for the therapist to stop playing and to listen. As we have already seen, there is no right or wrong way.

Frank, an elderly man with mild learning difficulties and a long history of depression, came to an assessment music therapy session. One of the first instruments he approached was a bass xylophone. He played some sounds upon it, at a moderate speed but with no apparent rhythmic pattern or melody. The therapist answered with random notes of her own on the piano, but felt very little connection with Frank's music – he seemed far away in his own world. She realised that her task as therapist was simply to stay with him, also making sounds, and tolerating the sense of distance between them. After a while, Frank looked up and said:

'I used to play one like this a long time ago, when I was at boarding school. I wish that I could remember the tunes the music teacher used to teach us.'

He then continued playing and, a few moments later, stopped again and said: 'Can you teach me?' The therapist, also stopping, answered: 'Let's take our time and try to get to know one another before we make any plans.'

They then both continued playing.

During this short extract from a session during the assessment phase of the music therapy, the therapist responded to the client (whom she hardly knew) by playing when he played, but stopping to listen when he stopped to say something. Here Frank's words were both a means of self-expression, almost as part of the music but also a way for him to make contact. The therapist was not following any set formula in stopping and starting her music; she was simply trying to pick up cues from Frank that might help her to get to know him better. She heard both the words and the music as part of his involvement in the session and was listening to the expressive quality of each.

Clients who Prefer to Talk

For child and adult clients who usually communicate through words and where client and therapist share the same language, spoken conversation will naturally form part of sessions. In many settings, where clients speak quite spontaneously or are talkative, verbal interaction may play a greater part than in the session with Frank. Here the therapist may also use words to help to explore their joint understanding of what might be happening during the sessions. For example, the therapist might want to find out more about the client's experience of the music so might ask, 'I wonder how you are feeling?' or 'That music sounded very sad to me and I'm wondering if you too are feeling sad?'.

Pavlicevic writes: 'In early sessions the depth and immediacy of contact as well as the sharp focus of emotional experience may be frightening. Here the therapist may need to check verbally, the patient's experiences and feelings' (1990: 8). This 'checking' can be extremely important when working with clients whom the therapist does not know very well or who seem to have become particularly distressed during a session. Spontaneous questions after improvising can also enable the client to be guided by the therapist into a more reflective part of himself or herself but where this is actively rejected by the client, it may indicate that words are not relevant, or not at this particular moment. It is sometimes helpful to think of a client's non-verbal response to the therapist speaking as part of the process of inter-personal exploration; the tension of silence as a response to words can be an important communication.

In some instances, it can be hard to engage clients in playing music, particularly in the early stages of the therapy when they may prefer to talk instead, gradually gaining enough confidence to try the instruments. How can we understand a client's preference for words and reluctance to play? Does this mean that they are not suitable for music therapy or might they benefit instead from a talking therapy such as counselling or psychotherapy? Will music therapy merely serve to increase their anxiety if, for some reason, they feel unable to make musical sounds? These questions have no clear-cut answers. When some clients refuse to play, preferring to speak, it can seem to be a form of resistance to engaging in music therapy, which the therapist might understand as being part of a process. Simpson (2000: 83–92), in his research into the place and significance of verbal communication, identifies different types of verbal interaction, some of which may facilitate and enhance the therapeutic process while others might dilute or hinder it. The therapist has to work hard to hold the belief in their minds that the client is indeed suitable for music therapy and that choosing not to play is also a way of relating. There may be a purpose (as yet unknown) in allowing the client to wait to engage musically until they feel ready. The music therapist whose client chooses not to play may experience some uncomfortable but important feelings, which can be considered in terms of countertransference. The therapist may feel rejected, undervalued, marginalised, manipulated, ineffective and de-skilled. They may feel guilty that they are being paid to do 'music therapy' and yet there is no music. 'Another music therapist would have got the client to play from the start,' might be their thought. If the therapist can think about these feelings dynamically in terms of a countertransference communication from the client, it may lead to accessing the problems that the client is bringing to the therapy. For example, that the client might be anxious about whether the therapist is good enough to help them, or may feel unable to trust the therapist enough to reveal their own perceived inadequacy.

The Issue of Musical Skill

In Chapter 1 we described a music therapy workshop where participants had come to find out more about the use of music as therapy and this may well have included the invitation to take part in a group improvisation. We saw how people were generally able to speak freely about their experience of music and their relationship to it. These same people, however, may have experienced a sudden onset of anxiety, when they were asked to play an instrument freely with a group of strangers. For some, the free nature of the workshop music-making would have been in direct contrast to everything they had ever been taught about playing an instrument. For others, the music-making would evoke memories of early negative musical experiences at school or a failed attempt at piano lessons. It might feel very hard for people to play at all if they had rarely or never taken part in music before. However, for others, the freedom of being invited to take part in an instant musical event could evoke immense excitement. All the participants in such a workshop situation are taking an enormous leap into the dark, carrying with them their musical histories. Although attending a workshop is a very different experience, adult clients coming to music therapy, particularly during initial sessions, frequently express similar feelings in response to free improvisation, ranging from anxiety to excitement. Their adult relationship to music may be coloured by memories of musical education, acquired musical skills, perceived lack of musical skill, personal taste in music, views about what is and what is not music and, most frequently, intense attachment to a particular piece of music. Most clients who come to music therapy speak positively of their relationship to music, particularly of music to which they like listening or dancing. Nevertheless, frequently their relationship to actually playing music involves feelings that are more difficult. This may be in part because in Britain at the start of the twenty-first century we still generally regard music as the province of experts. Music is often considered as something to be listened to, live in a concert hall or on compact disc, rather than as an active shared experience. Pavlicevic recounts her experience in Johannesburg where in a piazza she heard an outdoor performance of drummers from Mozambique. She writes:

> What soon became evident was the cultural differences between people's experiences of the music. The Africans seemed to go on their daily business, hawking, talking, walking past, almost as though the music were not occurring. Some occasionally joined the drummers and the dancers for a short burst and would then leave and continue on their daily business. In contrast, the non-Africans sat and listened to the music, mostly in silence, as though it were a concert performance. For some people, music was part of the day and you simply went about your business, whereas for others it was a separate event. (1997: 35)

The issue of musical skill is a focus for some clients throughout their time in music therapy. It is often expressed through criticism of their own music, as though clients have an internal voice, sitting in judgement on their every musical move. Some typical responses of these clients to the improvised music may include:

- I **can't** play – I have no skill.
- I **can't** play but you (therapist) **can** play, you are the professional.
- I **can't** play but you (therapist) and the rest of the group **can** play.
- I **can't** play and neither can any of us (other group members), but you **can** play so please will you teach us something?

Primrose, a 52-year-old woman who attended a music therapy group in a mental health day hospital over a two-year period, would harangue the therapist and the other group members angrily with her views about their music. She would say, for example:
'This isn't music, all this banging, it is just a noise!'
'This isn't playing, you need to learn how to play the instruments properly.'
'Give me six months and I'll probably be able to play this metallaphone.'

It was as though she could only consider herself within music therapy in relation to her perception of the level of musical skill in the group. She constantly measured her musical abilities in relation to others, mostly comparing herself unfavourably, and appeared to be unable to let herself go and simply play. However, the therapist began to understand that Primrose's responses to the music reflected feelings that were buried deep inside her. Her anger with the therapist for allowing her to feel so vulnerable in playing music seemed to the therapist to reflect her anger at being so dependent on others to take of her. The disgust she expressed at the harsh and discordant 'banging' of the music seemed to reflect the pain, which was hard for her to acknowledge, of the harsh reality of her mental illness. Instead, she needed to dismiss it as 'noise' and 'not music'. To the therapist these seemed to be important issues to work through together over an extended period. Primrose was communicating the pain and anger which had long been part of her life through the metaphor of musical skill.

Margaret was a widow in her mid-80s who now lived alone in the flat she had shared with her husband (who had recently died) for over 38 years. She was referred to a music therapy group, which took place in a mental health day hospital for older adults. She had attended the day hospital for five months prior to her referral as she was undergoing assessment of her cognitive state. It was likely that she had mild/moderate senile dementia, but due to her difficulty in expressing herself verbally, it had been hard to engage her in groups which involved talking, and therefore to carry out the assessment. She was evidently experiencing severe difficulty in finding words, which made her feel very anxious and foolish. Non-verbally, however, she was extremely communicative, both in her movements and in her facial expressions, and she seemed to gain pleasure from being with people.

At the initial assessment session in which Margaret was alone with Rob, the therapist, she chose a drum and they began to play together. At first, Margaret made light, tentative tapping sounds as though reluctant to engage with the instrument, but as she became more confident, she moved into playing dance-like rhythmic patterns, which interacted with Rob's playing. After they had finished the session, Margaret asked Rob, anxiously, if he knew what was wrong with her. Although she was experiencing some degree of short-term memory loss and might have forgotten what she had been told, the therapist wondered if her question was a way of finding out if he understood what she was going through in losing her faculties, and how frightening this felt.

Following this session, Margaret became a regular member of a music therapy group, but after some weeks she still kept referring back to the playing that had taken place during the assessment session. She was very concerned that her music might now be getting 'worse'. The therapist understood that this was her way of expressing feelings about the loss of her cognitive functioning as a result of dementia.

As a young adult, Margaret had been a dancer and had then become a dancing teacher. She had a well-developed relationship with music which was expressed through her musical sensitivity and the coherent way in which she responded musically to others. However, in the same way that she felt humiliated by her struggle to articulate what she wanted to say in words, it seemed that she also felt distressed at losing some of her musical skills. She was extremely critical of every sound she made, often pointing to the piano in the music room and saying sadly, **'That's** what I used to do'. She frequently suggested that she should leave the group, as 'This might be better for everybody'. Rob responded by asking her if she was finding the *group too hard. On another occasion, he suggested that, maybe, she thought that she was not wanted in the group, or that she thought the others were critical of her contributions. The therapist gradually came to the conclusion that she really did want to stay in the group, but that she needed much reassurance. After three months (which included a two-week Christmas break) she began to settle, and to play the instruments. Her playing began to feel more connected to the group's music as a whole, and she was apparently having no difficulty with concentration. There was a significant new development when, with the encouragement of the others in the group, she began to dance to the music. Her agility and her degree of self-expression whilst dancing was remarkable. It seemed that she was now contributing an extremely important part of herself to the group. Although she remained concerned that 'she was not good enough' to be in the group, she was now far more relaxed and enthusiastic about coming. The music therapy group came to an end with the therapist's departure from the hospital. As they spoke in the group sessions about the ending, Margaret became more anxious again and concerned about her lack of ability. She did, however, manage to say goodbye to Rob in the final session in a way that felt meaningful, looking him straight in the eye, and emphasising by her tone of voice that she understood that the sessions were finishing. She seemed to be conveying that, despite her prevailing anxiety about being good enough, coming to sessions had meant something positive to her.*

Turry makes it clear that the therapist, too, may have issues about musical skill which can impede the therapeutic process. He describes a situation where the session was being recorded on video, with the agreement of the client, for the therapists' personal study. Turry writes:

> The client was a gifted musician who felt that verbal psychotherapy was not right for him. During the initial meeting, we began to improvise together, and a vague discomfort began to grow in me. I was not satisfied with what I was playing. It sounded satisfying musically, but I did not feel connected to the client with whom I was playing. I began to feel I was being judged and became extremely self-conscious. I questioned whether I was a good enough musician in my client's eyes.
>
> This feeling continued until he asked me if we could stop the video recording of the session. I wondered if his request indicated that he, too,

felt he was being judged. Once I considered this, my music changed from being complex and sophisticated to being more sparse, more receptive, and, in a sense, less competitive with his ... my own issues with competition and being good enough were so close to his that it took the reflection offered by his request to help me to realize that my feelings were conveying aspects of the client's life in addition to being a result of my own history. (1998: 190–91)

Symbolic Play in Music Therapy

As we have already seen in Chapter 4, 'playing' in music therapy can involve more than playing the instruments. Children can use the freedom of the therapy room to play games and act out stories, both of which involve using the instruments symbolically. A scenario which frequently occurs when there is a grand piano in the music room, is when a child crawls under the piano. This could be for a variety of reasons, for example:

- to play hide-and-seek with the therapist;
- to make a pretend house;
- to feel safe in an enclosed space;
- to pretend to go to sleep;
- to avoid the therapist; or
- to withdraw from activity.

How the therapist joins in the game will be a personal choice, depending on the stage of the therapy and the therapist's perception of the reasons behind it. In Pablo's therapy, his imaginative games told the therapist a great deal both about his inner world and about some of the ordeals to which he and his family had been subjected in the war situation from which they had recently escaped.

This is an extract from a longer case study; see Tyler (2002).

Pablo

After the long summer break, Pablo was eager to come to his sessions and wanted to 'get on with the game' as soon as he came in. The music room became transformed each week into a variety of dramatic settings: a bench became the court-room, a locked cupboard was the prison, inside which were the tigers. There was also a palace, a castle, a jungle and a river. There were cages, searchlights and security cameras, electric wires and bombs but also magic spells and sleeping potions. The instruments and the room took on new guises as follows:

Windchimes	= *magical powers*
Tambourines	= *protective shields*
Metal beater	= *screwdriver to connect the electricity*
Cupboard	= *cage full of tigers*
Whistle	= *for taming tigers*
Drum-sticks	= *swords*
Bass drum	= *a signal*
High-hat cymbal	= *crocodile's teeth*
Swanee whistle	= *for shooting arrows or a laser gun*
Video camera	= *security lights or cctv*

The tortures with which Pablo threatened his prisoners included hungry lions, electric shocks and the eating of limbs by the crocodile. While some of these are familiar themes in children's fiction and fairy-tales (such as 'Red Riding Hood', Barry's 'Peter Pan' or Sendak's 'Where the Wild Things Are'), they also demonstrate the level of his sense of persecution and his premature knowledge of real-life torture. Pablo's dramatic stories can be understood as a personal expression of his traumatic experiences. The fantasies of aggression and destruction which are a normal part of child development were to him a frightening and horrible reality.

So what had happened to the music? Was this now a form of play therapy, using musical instruments as props in the game, and was the music merely like a film score, highlighting moments of drama? This was a question the therapist pondered both in the sessions and during supervision, particularly as Pablo became more controlling in defining the musical limits of the session. Despite his frequent efforts to silence the music, however, the therapist felt that the music had brought them to this point and it therefore continued to be a vital ingredient, either in its presence or absence.

8

MUSIC THERAPY WITH ADULTS: FOUR CASE STUDIES

In this second chapter of case studies we are going to focus upon four people who took part in music therapy, and show how their particular histories and current needs shaped the course of the therapy. We will describe how the music therapists adapted their music therapy skills to meet each client as an individual and how they used music therapy and psychotherapy literature to support their thinking about their work.

Robert

The lounge was spacious, with a soft carpet and comfortable chairs. Sunlight streamed in through French windows, beyond which were well-kept grounds, laid out with grass and trees. Although music was blaring from a large television set, the room seemed empty, but on looking more closely the small figure of Robert could be seen, curled up on the floor with his head tucked into his arms, apparently asleep.

It was Helen's first day as a music therapist in a NHS residential unit for 20 adults with profound and multiple disabilities. The manager of the unit, Ruth, who was showing her round, explained that most of the residents went to a day centre, but there were a few, including Robert, who stayed behind, and they would be her music therapy clients.

Robert had little to occupy him, spending much of the day dozing in the television lounge, and Ruth was very keen that he should have music therapy because he apparently responded to music and would sing along with well-known tunes.

When Helen went to fetch him for his first session, which was to be held in the games room along the corridor, he was extremely reluctant to leave the comfort of his usual position and needed much encouragement and support from Ruth. Once in the room, alone with Helen, he sat on a chair with his legs tucked under him, gazing impassively into the distance. She introduced herself and showed him the instruments, the piano, drum, cymbal, tambourine and bells, explaining that they were for making music together but that he did not need to play unless he wanted to. There was a silence, which Helen broke by beginning to sing softly and play the piano. Robert gave no indication that he had heard her, continuing to gaze ahead. She noticed that he had a habit of moving his head from side to side in a slow, shaking movement and this gave her something to reflect in the music and a tempo in which to play. She also saw that his knuckles were covered with scars and scabs, as though they had been recently injured.

After a few minutes, he slipped off his chair, curled up on the floor and apparently fell asleep. Helen continued to sing for a little while, then sat quietly, feeling increasingly sleepy herself. Her intuition was not to try to rouse Robert with loud or lively music, but to remain alongside him, tuning in to his physical and emotional state. They remained together like this for the next half hour, Helen occasionally singing or playing an instrument gently, and Robert showing no response. It was as though her music had replaced the sounds from the television in providing a background for his half-sleeping, half-waking reverie.

The second session was a week later, and again Helen had to wake Robert and help him to walk along the corridor. Once in the room, to her surprise, he immediately pushed the drum and the cymbal over with some force and hurled the tambourine across the room. He then took up his position on the chair, once again appearing impervious to any sounds she made. Again, she used the music to reflect his various body movements, as he sat flicking his fingers or tapping his knee. However, at the end of the session, when she began to improvise a lyrical 'goodbye' song, Robert could be heard singing softly in a falsetto voice, following the contours of the melody. He had now shown two contrasting parts of himself, the passive, withdrawn person with the sweet singing voice, and the energetic aggressive man, who could show his strength in unpredictable bursts of anger.

Robert was in his early thirties. He was non-verbal with microcephaly, epilepsy and partial sight and he needed assistance when walking. He had been born with severe brain damage and had lived in a children's hospital from the age of two, after his mother who was chronically depressed had committed suicide. He moved to his current accommodation in his late teens and plans were being made for another move, to a smaller supported home. Although he was described as generally passive and 'no trouble', he would bite his hands, drawing blood, and had occasional outbursts of violent behaviour during which he would bang doors with great force or break a window with his fist. He would also try to tip over wheelchairs or destroy anything resembling a hospital trolley, and this had led to him being excluded from the day centre. No one knew what caused these episodes, but Helen was assured by the manager that it would not affect the therapy as he 'loves music.'

This last comment reflects a common misperception about music therapy for adults with learning disabilities. Carers or professionals may see it as an entertainment, a way of passing the time pleasantly or as an activity which should bring out the best in people and therefore discourage difficult or challenging behaviour. 'He loves music' is a common reason for referral, reflecting the wish to improve the quality of life for people who may be very restricted in their opportunities for enjoyable activities. Ansdell writes:

> Most music therapists have suffered at some point from being put down as a glorified entertainer, just as most psychotherapists will have been asked whether they are really better than finding a friend to talk to when you have a problem. Which is not to say that entertainment is *not* part of music therapy – playing music with another person is indeed often entertaining and joyous. But whatever the character of the experience, it happens, as does the verbal dialogue of psychotherapy, within a sustained, secure and dependable relationship … Music is a powerful phenomenon as entertainment pure and simple. It is also a powerful agent within the specific context of therapy. (1995: 35)

The consequence of working with this 'powerful agent' is to accept the expression of emotions such as grief, loss, frustration, anger and depression (all of which may have been experienced by Robert), and therefore to acknowledge that a person with profound disabilities is capable of having an inner life. This was an issue recognised by a group of colleagues at the Tavistock Clinic in London in the late 1970s and 1980s, when they set up workshops to explore the use of psychotherapy with patients described in the terminology of the day as 'mentally handicapped' (Sinason, 1992: 40). This challenged the opinion that a client would need to possess sophisticated verbal skills in order to benefit from psychotherapy and recognised the concept of a distinction between 'cognitive intelligence and emotional intelligence' (Stokes and Sinason, 1992: 51). In a similar way, the music therapist works with the client's innate musical emotional intelligence, which, as we have seen already, is not dependent on musical knowledge or skill.

As Robert's therapy continued, Helen noticed that he walked more steadily and purposefully along the corridor. In his sessions, which lasted 45 minutes, he continued to alternate between sitting on the chair or lying half-asleep on the floor, but the moments when he joined in with singing became gradually more extended. If Helen placed an instrument near him, however, he would push it over or throw it away decisively.

In the ninth week of therapy, he began to hum fragments of a melody as he approached the music room. Helen answered him, singing his name, and a dialogue developed which continued as they entered the room. For the first time Robert was not 'joining in', or 'singing along' but creating and sharing the melody in a communicative, interactive dialogue. He showed a finely-tuned sense of pitch and rhythm, holding a low bass note on the dominant (or fifth degree) of the key in which they were singing, and then improvising an exuberant descant above Helen's melody. He was not using words but repeated sounds such as ma-ma, ba-ba and da-da-da. Listening to a tape recording of the session afterwards, it was clear that these sounds were like those of an infant in a tender conversation with a parent.

Assessing Robert after the first three months, it was clear that he was beginning to trust the therapy setting and the developing relationship, despite his rejection of the instruments. Helen's ongoing aim was to help him to bring all of himself into the music, so that the angry and frustrated part could be voiced and heard musically, rather than expressed through destructive or self-injurious outbursts.

As Robert's singing became increasingly confident and interactive, he began, significantly, to use a deep voice as well as his usual falsetto. Helen began to support him by playing a drum, rather than the piano and this he accepted without needing to push it away. She then found a way of helping him to play it: first she would beat the drum to the rhythm of their singing, using the flat of her hand, then she would stop singing and playing, holding her hand above the drum. Robert's wish for the music to go on was so great that he would take Helen's wrist and, using her hand as a beater, continue to beat vigorously. On the first occasion he used such force that her hand went through the skin of the drum. Over a period of several weeks, and by Helen using the same method, Robert was able to move on to playing with a beater (which Helen held firmly in her hand) until he was eventually able to hold it and play by himself. The music became lively and full of energy, and there was a sense of humour in some of their exchanges as Robert chuckled and shouted as he played the drum. The instruments were still frequently pushed over and at other times he would retreat into sleep, but it was clear that he was enlivened by the music. Ansdell describes this process as 'quickening', using the term 'to suggest the way in which music works therapeutically not by giving a mechanical stimulus but by somehow lending some of its qualities of liveliness and motivation to both body and spirit' (1995: 81).

Helen worked with Robert for only 10 months before his unit was closed, but in that time there had been marked developments. At first it had seemed that he chose not to communicate, and isolated himself by his non-responsiveness and falling asleep. He appeared to feel most comfortable in the role of a baby, curled up safely, with a lullaby to soothe him. When we consider the traumatic loss of both his mother and his home at the age of two it is understandable that he retreated into this safe cocooned world and was angry and fearful when made to leave it. As he came to trust the therapy, he was able to risk exploring the grown-up aspects of himself – first as a form of resistance (throwing and pushing) and eventually discovering his mature voice both in singing and in using his strength to play. The changes in the sessions were paralleled by changes in him noted by the staff, such as increased alertness and improved ability to make choices.

Robert's life story, with his moves from long-stay hospital into a smaller residential unit and eventually to resettlement in a home in the community, reflects changing government policies over the second half of the twentieth century. As we saw in Chapter 5, the Education Act of 1970 reflected new attitudes towards children with disabilities. In 1971 a Government White Paper *Better Services for the Mentally Handicapped* sought to bring about similar changes in the lives of adults. The main thrust of this White Paper was to reduce the number of places in long-stay hospitals and to increase provision in the community. Thirty years later, a new White Paper, *Valuing People: A New Strategy for Learning Disability for the 21st Century*, looked at what had been achieved and outlined plans for the future (DOH, 2001). Among statistics we can read that in 1969 there were 58,850 patients resident in NHS hospitals and units and 4,900 in residential care homes. By 2000 the numbers had changed significantly, with 10,000 remaining in NHS provision and 53,400 in residential care. These radical changes have affected the work of the many music therapists employed by the large institutions in the 1960s, 70s and 80s. The well-established music therapy departments were no longer needed for the residents, and so the therapists either diversified into other developing areas of music therapy (such as forensic psychiatry) or were re-deployed in the community. The patients remaining in the long-stay hospitals tended to be either very elderly or with profound and complex needs.

The second case study introduces music therapy which took place within a Day Centre run by the Social Service Department of an inner city borough. The Centre employed part-time music therapist, Helen, for one day each week. The 14 service users, whom the staff referred to as students, were young adults with severe learning difficulties who had been to school in the borough and now were receiving further education and social skills training. The majority of the students were non-verbal, several had challenging behaviour, and all except one lived in supported accommodation provided by the social services. Thirty years earlier they would have almost certainly been living in hospitals, possibly far from their place of origin. The policy of Care in the Community allowed them to remain in the district in which they had been brought up, with the service provision changing appropriately as they moved from child to adult. At the Day Centre the students were given sessions in self-care, cooking, games, art, gardening, dance and aromatherapy massage, with trips to the pub, park, cinema, swimming pool or café. In the summer there were holidays and special outings, while winter brought a spate of Christmas parties. As with all groups, some people were sociable in nature and thrived on the active environment of the Day Centre, but there were several who clearly found it a stressful place to be. One man paced up and down endlessly and would not join in with group activities, while another would get upset, screaming or hitting out, if people came too close. Louise, however, was the student who caused the staff most concern because of her apparent depression, and so when a space became available in Helen's timetable, she was immediately referred for sessions.

Louise

Louise was a young woman of 24 with epilepsy and severe learning disabilities. As a child she had lived with her parents and attended a special school, but her mother became ill and it became increasingly difficult for her father to care for Louise at home. When she was eight her mother died and Louise was placed in a boarding school. At school-leaving age she moved to a community home and began to attend the Day Centre. She still had contact with her father, although this became less as the years went on. Care staff said that she was always excited when her father came, but after his visits she would become depressed, standing by the window for long periods, sometimes crying silently. Similarly, she would show sadness when familiar staff members left their jobs at her home or the Day Centre (as they frequently did) and would seem to be waiting for them to come back, standing by the window.

In the Day Centre Louise tended to be isolated, sitting alone and moving away if anyone approached her, or walking around lethargically, with slow, dragging steps. She would allow staff to lead her and guide her into activities, but she needed one-to-one encouragement and assistance. The exception to this was anything connected to eating, and Louise frequently went to the fridge to look for food.

Louise had no speech but vocalised repetitively. Slumped in an armchair, her legs crossed tightly, arms folded and hands tucked under her armpits, she would repeat a descending melodic phrase over and over again. The register was low, from middle C, descending a fifth to low F and the sound seemed to come from deep in her throat. She did not seem to use the sounds to communicate with other people in the room, but rather it seemed to be a way of isolating herself still further.

Janet Graham, researching into the non-verbal communication of clients, describes 'grunting, mouth-clicking, snorting and repetitive shouts' and suggests that:

> These sounds appear to have become habitual and often now seem intended to protect their users from the communicative attempts of other people. Babbling sounds and melodic humming are also heard, and these, too, can appear to have become habitual. Perhaps they were once intended to communicate but, after continual failure to be heard and responded to, have gradually become a self-reassuring habit and ultimately a social barrier. (2000: 3)

This is how Helen, the music therapist, perceived Louise's vocal sounds, and, after observing and hearing her in the Day Centre, she looked forward to starting work with her, feeling that she was already making a potential musical offering.

The room used for music therapy was very small, opening off the main lounge where general activities took place. It was sparsely furnished, with a piano, a couple of chairs and the musical instruments. Louise passively accepted being led to the room, but after one glance, walked straight out again and stood by the window of the lounge with her back to Helen, vocalising loudly. She determinedly resisted Helen's efforts to persuade her to come back to the music room. It was the same the second week, Louise leaving immediately and making it very clear that she would not stay in the room. Again, she vocalised loudly and clearly, with a distinct falling melody, but Helen was inhibited from answering her because of the other students and staff in the lounge. Having observed her wandering freely around the Day Centre, Helen was aware that to be enclosed in a small room with a stranger must feel quite threatening and overwhelming. After three weeks of this frustrating impasse the problem was solved when Helen was able to rearrange the session to a time when the large lounge was not being used. Now Louise would be able to come in and out of the music room, leaving the door open, without being disturbed or disturbing anyone.

The fourth session began with Louise accepting being led into the music room and vocalising strongly. Helen answered her, singing 'Hello, Louise' to the same tune. Louise picked up a stick which was lying on the drum and began to beat slowly and heavily. Her grip was loose, as though she could not commit herself to a firm beat, and the stick rebounded each time she played. As Helen tried to join the tempo of her beating from the piano she dropped the stick on the floor, as though she could not be bothered to hold it, and walked out of the room to the lounge. This time Helen did not follow her but stayed at the piano, her improvising reflecting the tempo of Louise's dragging footsteps and her vocal sounds which now seemed to have a distressed and choking quality. Helen wondered if she felt pressurised or whether the musical reflecting of her sounds was touching her emotionally. It was apparent that Louise needed to put a physical distance between them, but she made no attempt to leave the lounge area.

Before the next session, Helen moved the drum into the lounge, near the music room door, and placed an armchair nearby so that the lounge became an extension of the therapy room. This seemed to reassure Louise, who again played for brief periods and vocalised in her familiar way. She made no eye contact, as she usually stood with her back to Helen or out of sight in the lounge but there was a musical link between them through the vocalising and the drum beating. Louise's responses were intermittent and unpredictable, stopping as suddenly as they began; nevertheless she seemed to be aware of being answered, both vocally and from the piano. For example, her vocal sounds were not fixed; if Helen changed key, moving to a higher pitch, Louise's vocal sounds would also change. This indicated that although she seemed unable to tolerate the intensity of the relationship within a confined space, she was not impervious to musical communication.

As Louise became accustomed to the timing of the sessions, and perhaps more trusting in Helen as a reliable figure, she began to attend more readily. It became possible to bring the armchair and the drum back into the room and to shut the door and so to have a contained and private place in which to work. It now seemed to Helen that Louise had possibly been trying for years to communicate through her vocal sounds but that she had not had the experience of being answered. By reflecting the sounds musically, Helen wanted to convey that she heard and recognised Louise's mood of heaviness and depression, but increasingly she found that she too was being drawn into it, so that the music between them became ever more oppressively despondent.

One way of thinking about what was happening between Helen and Louise is in terms of countertransference. Helen not only hears the musical attributes of Louise's vocalising in its pitch, melody, phrase structure and rhythm, but also listens to her own musical response to 'get a deeper sense of the client's experience' (Streeter, 1999: 15). This inner listening then enables her to make the musical change or intervention which is necessary and to know when it is the right moment.

The moment of change happened quite spontaneously in the ninth session. The music had seemed to be going round and round in circles as Helen reflected back Louise's repetitive sounds. Then Helen stopped playing and singing, and sat listening, wondering what she should do. At that moment, the music that came into her mind was the song known as Brahms' Lullaby (opus 49, no. 4). After a pause, she began to play it, tentatively at first, singing without words. As the melody unfolded, Helen realised that by playing in F major (an instinctive choice of key), Louise's repetitive singing fitted exactly into Brahms' tune. Not only did the melody fit, but also Louise seemed to be timing her vocalising to co-ordinate with the rhythm and structure of the song. It felt to Helen that Louise already knew the song on a deep level and that it had meaning for her. This session proved to be the first significant point of meeting between the therapist and the isolated young woman, and the Lullaby became an important part of subsequent sessions.

So was it just a coincidence that Helen chose that music at that particular moment? What were the characteristics of the song which had called forth such a profound response from Louise? A lullaby has universal associations with the mother–child relationship, as a piece of music which conveys love, comfort and reassurance. This related to Helen's experience of the part of Louise which was still like a needy child, deprived of her mother and separated from her father. There was also, however, a strength in Louise which she seemed to have derived from the parental love and care which she had known in her early life. Her restless walking, gazing out of the window and her persistent vocal calls were perhaps a way of her searching for what she had once known. Helen was not attempting to become a substitute for the lost mother, but instead, through the relationship in the music, aimed to facilitate Louise to get in touch with the part of her which had received 'good enough mothering' (Winnicott, 1990: 145–6) in her early childhood, and to keep that part alive.

Louise's response to this particular piece of music was not an end in itself, but marked the start of a new phase in the therapy. The song provided a place where she could meet Helen, emotionally and musically, to mourn her many past losses and to have an alternative means of acknowledging her present depression. As Graham writes about the distressed sounds made by her non-verbal clients in a long-stay hospital:

> Staff sometimes regard these as habitual but I would suggest that they are expressive and communicative in intent. Perhaps the clients express

rage or despair with a world which makes little sense and which seems to have given up trying to listen to them. Perhaps they cry for the many losses they have experienced: loss of normality of intellect and body with the associated loss of independence; loss of privacy and any allowance for individuality; loss of family, home life and personal possessions, and loss of relationships with peers and care staff who have left them. (2000: 2)

The physical and intellectual damage to both Louise and Robert happened before birth, and the resultant emotional losses were experienced over a lifetime. The third case study is based on work with a musician whose life was changed in one day when a severe headache led to a brain haemorrhage, resulting in hemiplegia and loss of sight.

There is a developing interest in the effectiveness of music therapy within neurological rehabilitation, which includes patients with traumatic brain injury and strokes (Purdie, 1997: 45–50) as well as with patients who have a chronic neuro-degenerative disorder such as Huntingdon's Disease (Davis and Magee, 2001: 51–60). Purdie's research with patients who had disabilities resulting from strokes revealed that those who received music therapy showed improvement in the areas of 'communication, depression and anxiety ... as well as on motivation, social interaction, emotional stability and cooperation' (1997: 49). Purdie also refers to the phenomenon of musical ability remaining relatively intact, even after traumatic brain injury. She warns, however, that this does not necessarily make music therapy easier:

> Their pre-morbid musical experience may be considerable, and may either help or hinder the therapeutic process, depending on the severity of the injury and the degree of psychological adjustment following the injury. Advanced musical ability can sometimes be yet another source of frustration and another unwanted opportunity for the person to 'fail'. On the other hand, it can be a means of rediscovering an unaffected or relatively intact ability, if tackled sensitively. (1997: 46)

Martin

Martin was 35, a healthy and active man who taught music until a brain haemorrhage left him in a coma. He gradually regained consciousness but it was a year before he was able to leave the hospital's neurological rehabilitation unit to be looked after by his parents and a full-time carer. As a result of the stroke Martin was blind, confined to a wheelchair, had

short-term memory loss and very limited movement in his left
side. The occupational therapist had referred Martin to music
therapy, hoping that it would provide psychological support as
well as a creative outlet, as in hospital he had repeatedly
expressed the wish to play the piano again.

In the initial sessions of music therapy with the therapist, Richard, Martin was outwardly bright and cheerful, full of optimism about making a complete recovery. He would frequently say 'I can't play Bach or Beethoven at the moment because my left hand won't work, but at least I can sing some songs to cheer us up.' He would then proceed to sing 'If you're happy and you know it, clap your hands' and other popular songs, accompanying himself with his right hand on the piano. He sang each song repeatedly, while Richard listened. If he joined in playing, Martin would generally ask him to stop, implying that he was not as skilled a musician as Martin had once been. After a while, Richard suggested that they could play something different together, perhaps improvising using the percussion instruments. Martin at first was prepared to try, but soon dismissed the sounds as 'too harsh and ugly'. He went back to the piano and continued his repetitive singing, reminding Richard 'I used to be a very good pianist' and regretting the loss of use of his left hand. His aural perception was apparently unaffected by the brain damage, as he could sing in tune and locate all the notes he needed on the piano. He made it clear that he only wanted to play music in a major key, not 'sad minor' or 'ugly atonal' music. Between songs he kept up a stream of bright social conversation, saying how lucky he was to have such a good family and how things could have been much worse. His memory problems caused him to repeat himself a great deal and he did not seem to take in anything that Richard tried to contribute.

This desire to keep the contents of music therapy sessions in a safe, unthreatening place is not confined to people with neurological impairment. Tyler describes 9-year-old Joe as singing songs such as 'Old MacDonald had a farm' and, like Martin, 'If you're happy and you know it, clap your hands', while being very controlling of the therapist's participation. She writes:

> The mood created by these songs was one of false jollity in contrast to the reality of the tension in the room ... Part of the struggle was to help Joe to find his authentic voice ...
>
> Through the music I could reflect what I perceived to be his inner state, aiming to help him tolerate an expression of disturbing and sad feelings,

from which he wanted to dissociate, wanting only to identify with what he called 'nice, happy, jolly music'. (1998: 64–65)

As a relationship of trust developed in the sessions, Martin began to talk more openly about his condition, and admitted that he often felt frustrated, depressed and suicidal. However, he constantly tried to 'put on a brave face' for the sake of his mother who was caring for him. When he realised that music therapy was a place where he could express his feelings of sadness and loss without being told to 'cheer up', he stopped singing the relentlessly happy songs. Instead, he began to talk at length about his situation, often crying bitterly. He now refused to play the piano, or allow the therapist to play, saying it was too upsetting, and rejected the other instruments as 'not musical' or 'too painful'. For some weeks, the sessions contained virtually no music as Martin talked, repeatedly expressing his despair about his condition and all that he had lost. Instead of pouring out songs, Martin was now pouring out a stream of words to which Richard was expected to listen, but not to join in. He described himself as 'a disgusting lump of rubbish in a pushchair' and wished that he could kill himself. Richard found himself feeling impotent and frustrated in his inability to use music to help Martin express his pain or to facilitate any change. Martin denied having any anger at what had happened to him, saying that there must be a higher purpose to his suffering, but when Richard challenged this his comments were fiercely rejected and he was made to feel foolish and insensitive.

Sometimes, Martin would forget Richard's name or say that he thought he was the taxi driver. He had to work hard in his supervision sessions to understand that his feelings of being unskilled and worthless were precisely the feelings with which Martin was struggling. This phenomenon is described in the psychotherapeutic literature as projection. During this period, however, Martin began to feel some sensation returning to his left side and showed Richard that he could now raise his hand from his lap. Richard suggested that he could find out what sounds Martin's left hand could make on the piano if he lifted it up and dropped it onto the keyboard. At first he was horrified by the random, dissonant clusters of notes that emerged, saying that it sounded 'rubbish and disgusting' and reverted to playing some of his old song tunes with his right hand. However, he was also able to see that the music from the left side of his body was an authentic and spontaneous expression of the damaged part of himself with which he was struggling to come to terms. He and Richard were able to talk about these two contrasting musical sound worlds, personifying them as the 'Beauty and the Beast'. Martin began to value the exploratory and out-of-control sounds made by his left hand and could now risk allowing Richard to improvise with him. At the same time, his conversation moved from the 'here and now' of his current situation into reflecting on family issues that had been present before his illness and continued to cause stress. The idealisation of his past life and the longed-for complete recovery had given way to a more realistic acceptance of the difficulties of life and the development of some insight about his future prospects.

Joyce

In this last case study we are going to describe work with an elderly woman, Joyce who had severe dementia and almost no speech. She lived on a continuing care ward in a mental health unit, where Rachel, the music therapist, worked with her during the last year of her life.

In many such hospital and residential settings where elderly adults in the UK receive care, the sound of the television and radio is constant. To the outsider these sounds can often feel intrusive and irrelevant, making it even harder to communicate with relatives, friends or patients. It is noticeable that in wards where communication with patients is the hardest and physical dependency the greatest, that some electronic sound is almost always present. Why might this be?

It is common knowledge amongst those who live with and care for adults suffering from dementia that, even where the dementia is in its final stages, musical sounds still evoke responses. Exactly how this occurs is currently not clear, although the phenomenon is extensively documented in research literature. Brotons makes two suggestions: first, that the 'aesthetic nature of music in turn activates preserved brain structures, thereby allowing these people to connect with the outside world for certain periods of time' (Brotons, 2000: 62); she also suggests, within the context of a music therapy intervention, that it may be the 'interpersonal caring relationship established with a therapist [which is] responsible for eliciting the responses' (2000: 62). Sound and music may be provided in these hospital settings for many reasons, but essentially it is likely that the act of switching on the television or radio is justified on the basis that patients may like it and respond positively. It may also be that sound, whether verbal or musical, performs a function beyond that of providing news and entertainment, alongside which the patient's waking, bathing, eating, sleeping and other routine tasks of daily living take place. The persistent sounds of a radio or television, with their reminders of time passing, can create a secure link with the outside world, away from the intense anxiety of caring for patients or relatives.

It is not surprising that staff caring for older adults, who may have little information about their patient's life before coming into hospital, frequently know about their musical responses and preferences. It is on this basis that live music is often sought for patients with senile dementia or a referral is made to music therapy. In the case of Joyce, her strong attachment to music was commonly known and a sense of her life, prior to her developing senile dementia, could be gleaned through conversations with her husband.

Joyce had been living on the continuing care ward for nearly two years when her husband, Henry wrote to the new Ward Manager to enquire about the possibility of her being referred for music therapy. She had taken part in a music therapy group in the past, and also had been seen individually by a music therapy student. Now, in the late stages of Alzheimer's disease, Joyce had withdrawn into her own world, becoming very isolated, and ,Henry was concerned that she was not receiving sufficient musical stimulation.

Joyce had a lifelong attachment to music. As a young woman, during the Second World War, she had entertained troops, and immediately afterwards trained as a singer and dancer at a London college. She had spent the rest of her working life singing in West End shows.

Henry lived nearby the hospital and would visit most days on a regular basis. He had provided Joyce with a personal stereo cassette player and he frequently brought her tapes of music from their extensive collection of recordings. Rachel met with Henry and heard about his concerns for his wife and his wish for her to have some access to musical experiences. She began to work with Joyce on a weekly basis. She could walk a little at first, from the sitting room area of the ward to a side room, but she seemed to retain little memory of their sessions together from week to week. She took no interest in the simple

*percussion instruments which Rachel offered to her, probably
because she did not understand what they were. She did, however,
make vocal 'calling' sounds, often from the back of her throat,
with the pitch rising up and down. She also looked momentar-
ily interested in the instruments when Rachel played, but it
soon became clear that what she responded to most was Rachel
singing. Rachel began to sing songs which came into her head
quite spontaneously. Joyce would either smile and nod or she
would join in, vocalising freely. Rachel also began to improvise
vocally, matching Joyce's pitches, and sometimes providing
some musical structure from two simple chords played on the
guitar.*

Although it was unlikely that Joyce remembered the weekly visits,
it felt to Rachel as though some familiarity was being established
between them. She remembered her, and it was possible that Joyce
sensed that she knew her, and certainly that through music they had
something in common. It was quite hard for Rachel to hold on to this
idea all the time as Joyce might fall asleep, or barely respond for
entire sessions. Rachel arranged another meeting with Henry, who
was very positive in his response to Rachel's account of the sessions
and full of suggestions. Rachel felt from this meeting that there
might be mutual benefit in Henry joining the sessions too. The three
of them worked together for 10 months, up to the week of Joyce's
death.

Henry immediately began to bring songs that they had sung
together in younger days, mostly British and American songs, which
he brought with the words carefully written out for Rachel to sing.
Sometimes he brought music from Joyce's collection of sheet music.
As the months progressed Henry began to bring other personal
items, for example, the hand-written manuscripts of songs which
Joyce had arranged for the stage. He talked about their life
together, travelling to the United States, and the premières of shows
by well-known composers, conducted by the famous conductors of
the time. He also began to talk about how Joyce had first become ill,
and how the person he had known for so long had begun to change
forever. Joyce would take part in these sessions to varying degrees.
It astonished Rachel that the sessions lasted an hour, a length
of time she would normally consider far too long in such
circumstances. Sometimes Joyce would fall asleep, which at first
seemed to worry Henry until he realised that Rachel didn't feel that

they were 'wasting her time' if she 'didn't respond'. Occasionally she would say something, a short phrase, such as 'lovely, lovely, darling'. Often, though, the only sound from her would be the grinding of her teeth. Nevertheless, she would take part non-verbally; Rachel encouraged Henry to sing to her and she would occasionally give a bemused smile or 'join in' with her vocal sounds. Rachel sometimes responded to Joyce's sounds as before with free improvisation, using the guitar as an accompaniment. She would also sing songs as they occurred to her spontaneously, and would move freely between songs and improvised music, in addition to helping Henry to choose songs from his song sheets. Gradually, they built up a repertoire of musical possibilities, both pre-composed and improvised. Joyce's responses did not change very much except during the last two weeks when she slept through most of the sessions. The atmosphere changed over the months, with both Rachel and Henry becoming more relaxed in this therapeutic trio, where one member was increasingly absent. In the final session, Joyce hardly seemed aware of what was happening around her. Rachel and Henry, however, improvised and sung their repertoire of songs, and as usual left spaces for her response. At one moment she woke up and vocalised loudly whilst they were singing, before dropping asleep again. The following week Henry phoned Rachel to tell her of his wife's death, saying how kind everyone on the ward had been. They arranged to meet a few weeks later as a way of saying goodbye and finishing the work. Rachel felt in retrospect that the music therapy sessions had created a particular opportunity for this couple to be together during the last months in a way that could reflect some of the earlier times they had shared together, making and listening to music. This was a process that she felt privileged to have shared.

9

MUSIC THERAPY
RESOURCES AND
INFORMATION

The Oaktree Unit was part of a large urban hospital. The patients were elderly, frail and suffered from a wide range of conditions associated with old age, including senile dementia and Parkinson's disease. One part of the unit was a specially designated Stroke Rehabilitation Centre where people would stay as in-patients for six to eight weeks. During this time they would receive intensive rehabilitative care involving a multidisciplinary team of doctors, nurses, occupational therapists, physiotherapists, speech and language therapists and psychologists. Another part of the unit comprised a small day hospital which could be attended on a daily basis for continuing treatment, following discharge from the inpatient areas. The unit also had five long-stay wards where patients who were too frail or confused to live in their own home or a community home were cared for until the end of their lives. The manager of the Oaktree Unit saw a programme about music therapy on the television and wondered if employing a music therapist might be of benefit to the patients on the long-stay wards where some of the patients were agitated and many were withdrawn and depressed. She had noticed how the atmosphere changed when live music was played one day by a visiting group of young musicians. She spoke to the multi-disciplinary team and many agreed with her view. The speech therapist suggested that a music therapist might also help the patients in the Stroke Rehabilitation Centre, because she had observed that people who had difficulty speaking were able to sing words to songs quite easily. The physiotherapist said it would be ideal to work with a music therapist in the day hospital to help to motivate patients to move as they became bored with treatment over long periods of time. Both the medical consultant and the psychologist were concerned at how hard it was for the patients who had recently suffered a stroke to talk about their distress, or even begin to express some of their feelings of rage and helplessness. They suggested that individual music therapy sessions might offer some support and recognition for the crisis in which these patients found themselves. The occupational therapist, who also possessed some musical skills, returned the discussion to thinking about the needs of patients residing on the long-stay wards. She sometimes organised group singing sessions for patients, facilitating them with the help of nursing staff in the sitting room areas of the wards. She said that she was concerned that some patients seemed very isolated, that they appeared to be just wasting away in the corner, and that individual music therapy might help to restore some communication. She also wondered if a music therapist might be able to run a group for the patients and their relatives, who often seemed uneasy when visiting, particularly where their parent, partner or friend had severe dementia and there was no apparent means of communication.

The Manager felt pleased that her suggestion had received this positive response but was now left with the following questions:

- Where would she find out more about music therapy?
- How was she going to be able to justify bidding for funds for a new music therapy service when there were so many acute needs to be met?

The future of the music therapy profession depends upon new services being set up and funded but this in turn depends on interested lay people deciding that they want to train and thus expanding the work of the profession. In this final chapter we are going to answer some typical questions and describe the resources that are available to inform the potential music therapy student, employer and manager alike.

Where can I find out about Music Therapy?

The British Society for Music Therapy (BSMT), mentioned throughout this book, is a special interest organisation open to all, whose aim it is to disseminate information about music therapy. The BSMT arranges conferences and workshops and also runs a specialist mail-order service for music therapy books and audio/video products. Further information about the BSMT can be found on their web-site www.bsmt.org or by writing to: BSMT Administrator, 25 Rosslyn Avenue, East Barnet, Herts. EN4 8DH, UK.

Who can benefit from Music Therapy?

Suitability for music therapy is not limited by age, disability, illness or health. As we have seen throughout this book a wide range of clients have benefited from a therapeutic relationship which is centred upon music. In Chapter 1 we described how music as a medium is part of human communication (including relationship and play), emotion (including self-expression), and movement. Wherever a clients' needs relate to communication, emotion or movement, music therapy may be a relevant intervention. For further reading, see:

- Bunt, L. and Hoskyns, S. (2002) *The Handbook of Music Therapy.* London: Brunner Routledge.
- Wigram, T., Nygaard Pedersen, I. and Bonde, L.O. (2002) *A Comprehensive Guide to Music Therapy.* London: Jessica Kingsley.

How do I know that it works? How can I find out about research?

As mentioned in earlier chapters, research has been a key factor enabling the growth of the profession and its statutory recognition, and is essential to its survival as a healthcare discipline. The accounts of clinical case material such as are contained throughout this book constitute a body of anecdotal evidence. Research is written about in some detail in the following publications:

- Bunt, L. (1994: 109–130) 'Music Therapy: An Art Beyond Words' *Music Therapy and Child Health – a survey of research* provides an account of Bunt's research projects with Children in London 1978–81. Here Bunt describes how he was able to show that 'music therapy can effect changes over a wide range of behaviours' (1994: 128).
- Heal, M. and Wigram, T. (eds) (1993), *Music Therapy in Health and Education.* Part II of this volume is devoted to descriptions of individual research projects that took place in the early 1990s

in Europe, Australia and the US. It includes an overview of research and a literature analysis by Tony Wigram, who charts the progress of music therapy research during the 1970s–90s, with particular reference to the UK and the US. Chapters include work with both children and adults.

Two other volumes that appeared in the early 1990s are devoted entirely to research and include chapters representing the work of all four arts therapies disciplines:

- Gilroy, A. and Lee, C. (eds) (1995) *Art and Music Therapy and Research*. This book includes music therapy research with adult offenders (Hoskyns: 1995), adults with profound learning difficulties (Oldfield and Adams, 1995), and cerebral palsied children (Van Colle and Williams, 1995). It also includes a chapter by Pavlicevic examining the interface for music therapy between music and emotion, and a chapter by Lee (1995) describing his research into the links between the musical therapeutic process and outcome, through detailed analysis of clinical improvisation. His client group were adults living with HIV and AIDS. Sutton (1995) describes the process of her research project into the sound-world of speech-and-language-impaired children.
- Payne (1993) *Handbook of Inquiry in the Arts Therapies* includes a directory of arts therapies research which was either completed or ongoing at the time. There are four arts therapies professions represented: art, music, drama, and dance-movement. Music therapy chapters include Wigram's research into the 'Effect of Music and Low Frequency Sound in Reducing Anxiety and Challenging Behaviour in Clients with Learning Difficulties' (Wigram, 1993). Levinge (1993) writes about her research using the ideas of Winnicott in music therapy with children and describes her personal process of undertaking the project. Rogers (1993) describes her research into music therapy with sexually abused clients.

Research from the 1990s and clinical case material about music therapy with the elderly is described in Aldridge (ed.) (2000). Here Brotons (2000) provides an overview of research into music therapy with this client group in the US, Vink (2000) summarises research which supports the use of music where elderly people are agitated in long-stay care settings. G. Aldridge (2000) gives an account of using an assessment procedure based upon a standard test for dementia.

Such evidence can also be found in many of the journal articles, conference proceedings and other publications about music therapy, which are listed in the References section of this book.

The British Journal of Music Therapy is published bi-annually by the two music therapy organisations in the UK, the BSMT and the APMT. Its contents include clinical case studies, historical perspectives, discourse and research. It attracts written articles from music therapists working in many parts of the world. It is available as part of membership of the BSMT (see above) and by direct subscription. Its website is linked to the BSMT: www.bsmt.org

Some research articles that have appeared since the mid 1990s include:

- Odell-Miller (1995) 'Why provide music therapy in the community for adults with mental health problems', *British Journal of Music Therapy*, 9 (1): 4–10.
- Moss, H. (1999) 'Creating a new Music Therapy Post: An Evidence Based Research Project', *British Journal of Music Therapy*, 13 (2): 49–58.
- Bunt, L., Burns, S. and Turton, P. (2000) 'Variations on a Theme: The Evolution of a Music Therapy Research Programme at the Bristol Cancer Help Centre', *British Journal of Music Therapy*, 14 (2): 56–69.
- Stewart, D. (2000) 'The State of the UK Music Therapy Profession: Personal Qualities, Working Models, Support Networks and Job Satisfaction', *British Journal of Music Therapy*, 14 (1): 13–27.

The Journal of Music Therapy is a quarterly research-orientated publication, published by the American Music Therapy Association (AMTA). A look at any issue of this journal will demonstrate the long tradition of research in the US. Also published by the AMTA is the practice-orientated journal *Perspectives*. Further details of both these journals can be found on the AMTA's website, www.musictherapy.org/research.html or by writing to: American Music Therapy Association, Inc., 8455 Colesville Road, Suite 1000, Maryland 20910, USA.

For a comprehensive review of references to research in medical literature which supports music therapy clinical practice with all types of clients, see *Research News*, Spring 2000, compiled by David Aldridge for the website www.musictherapyworld. This website includes a European Register of Research.

For ongoing discourse and scholarly articles on music therapy research, clinical, historical, philosophical, cultural, and biological perspectives, the *Nordic Journal of Music Therapy* has become an international forum. The contents are mainly in English. It has an online discussion website, www.hisf.no/njmt.

See also www.voices.no the free international on-line journal, also from Norway, which is updated fortnightly and includes informal discussion as well as articles. For research into the psychology of music, including music therapy, see *Journal of the Society for Education, Music and Psychology Research*: www.sagepub.co.uk/journals/details/j0469.html.

How is a Music Therapist employed?

Music Therapy is a state-registered profession with a protected title under the Health Professions Council. Music Therapists are registered as 'Arts Therapists (Music)' or SRAsT(M). This means that only those having successfully undertaken recognised training may call themselves a 'music therapist'. The APMT can provide information regarding the professional code of ethics and standards of practice. They can provide advice and other information covering all aspects of employing a music therapist.

To contact the APMT administrator, email APMToffice@aol.com.

The Health Professions Council can provide detailed information for employers and the general public about what a state registered practitioner can be expected to provide. Their website also enables a check on an individual's state registration status: www.hpcuk.org

How can I advertise for a music therapist?

The Association of Professional Music Therapists (APMT) (see above) publishes a monthly job circular (with the option of a five-day express service). This ensures that information about jobs is made known to all music therapists registered with the Association. As with State Registration, membership of the APMT is only open to music therapists who have undertaken recognised training.

I don't want to train as a music therapist but I want to develop my skills and work with people with special needs.

The community music association, Sound Sense, runs courses and workshops all over the UK and provides extensive information about music making opportunities and tuition for all (www.soundsense. org/). Also available, the Enquire Within service: tel. 01449 673990 or fax 01449 673994 or email info@soundsense.org. Alternatively write to: Sound Sense, 7 Tavern Street, Stowmarket, Suffolk. IP14 1PJ. UK.

I am not sure if I want to train as a music therapist but I would like to undertake a short course. Is this possible?

The BSMT organises regular day workshops and details of these can be found on their website. Throughout the UK in areas where music therapists are working, short introductory courses are frequently offered through colleges and universities and other adult education centres. It must be emphasised that these courses do not constitute music therapy training. They do, however, offer detailed information, the presentation of case material and experiential workshops in improvisation. They are ideal for those with an interest in training or in integrating interpersonal music-making into their current professional work, for potential employers, or those with a general interest such as musicians and academics. See the BSMT website for further information: www.bsmt.org.

Where can I find out about music therapy training courses?

The BSMT keeps up-to-date information about music therapy courses, which can be accessed via the BSMT website www.bsmt.org with links to each of the individual institutions offering training. In addition the training courses offer open days that give the potential student a chance to visit the institution and learn about application and interview procedures and what they can expect from the training.

Endnote – Some Final Thoughts

We end this book where we began in Chapter 1, with a group of people who scarcely know one another, who have been brought together because of their shared interest in music. This, however, is not a hospital music therapy session but a 'think-tank' of people who have come to share their views and experiences about the place of music in society in the twenty-first century.

When introductions are made, it is clear that most of the participants, including Helen, the music therapist, are actively involved in making or facilitating music with particular sections of society. There are representatives of music education, composers, music in hospitals, youth music, community music, music psychology, and performing musicians as well as music therapy. One man stands out as being different – he is a policeman, a chief constable. His brief is to report on the use of music in crime prevention, a sphere into which he has been researching. He tells the meeting about the experiments carried out around the country which show that when certain music is played in shopping malls or other public places the incidence of street crime by young people is considerably reduced. The experiment is encouraging the crime prevention service to look further into the use of music for this purpose.

In some ways, the policeman's story seems very different from those of the musicians who have been describing how they take their art to the disadvantaged, sick or needy. Yet it can also be seen that his particular professional experience of music brings it back into the heart of society, where it has always belonged.

Plato, in discussing his vision of the ideal state in *The Republic* (Plato, 1987: 98–103), saw music as a vital means towards moral and aesthetic growth. All the people gathered to discuss the role of music in society would have endorsed Plato's view that 'rhythm and harmony penetrate deeply into the mind and take a powerful hold on it'. In music therapy we have a chance to use this 'powerful hold' in a medium that is, at the same time, ancient and traditional but also constantly new and changing.

REFERENCES

Aigen, K. (1996) *Being in Music – Foundations of Nordoff–Robbins Music Therapy.* St Louis, MO: MMB Music.

Aigen, K. (1999) 'Welcome – Scientific Chair' in *Conference Programme, 9th World Congress of Music Therapy, Washington, November 1999.* American Music Therapy Association and World Federation of Music Therapy.

Aldridge, D. (ed.) (2000) *Music Therapy in Dementia Care.* London: Jessica Kingsley.

Aldridge, G. (2000) 'Improvisation as an Assessment of Potential in Early Alzheimer's Disease', in D. Aldridge (ed.), *Music Therapy in Dementia Care.* London: Jessica Kingsley. pp. 139–65.

Aldridge, D. and Brandt, G. (1991) 'Music Therapy and Alzheimer's Disease', *Journal of British Music Therapy*, 5 (2): 28–36.

Allen, R.E. (ed.) (1991) *Concise Oxford Dictionary.* Oxford: Oxford University Press.

Alvarez, A. (1992) *Live Company.* London and New York: Routledge.

Alvarez, A. and Reid, S. (1999) *Autism and Personality.* London: Routledge.

Alvin, J. (1965) *Music Therapy for the Handicapped Child.* Oxford: Oxford University Press.

Alvin, J. (1968) 'My Recent Tour Of Japan', *British Society for Music Therapy Bulletin*, 25: 11–16.

Alvin, J. (1975) *Music Therapy.* London: Hutchinson.

Alvin, J. (1978) *Music Therapy for the Autistic Child.* Oxford: Oxford University Press.

Ansdell, G. (1995) *Music for Life.* London: Jessica Kingsley.

Ansdell, G. (1997) 'Musical Elaborations, What has the New Musicology to say to Music Therapy?', *British Journal of Music Therapy*, 11 (2): 36–44.

Ansdell, G. (2002) 'Community Music Therapy and the Winds of Change – a Discussion Paper', in C. Kenny and B. Stige (eds) *Contemporary Voices in Music Therapy.* Oslo: Unipubforlag. pp. 109–142.

Association of Professional Music Therapists (1985) *A Handbook of Terms Commonly In Use In Music Therapy.* Cambridge: APMT Publications.

Association of Professional Music Therapists (1990) *A Career in Music Therapy.* Cambridge: APMT Publications.

Austin, D. (1998) 'When the Psyche Sings: Transference and Countertransference in Improvised Singing with Individual Adults', in K.E. Bruscia (ed.), *The Dynamics of Music Psychotherapy.* Gilsum, NH: Barcelona. pp. 315–33.

BBC (1976) Interview with Paul Nordoff in series: *Parents and Children*. London: BBC.

Benenzon, R.O. (1981) *Music Therapy Manual*. Springfield, IL: Charles C. Thomas.

Brahms, J. (c. 1864) *Wiegenlied*. Opus 49, No. 4.

Brotons, M. (2000) 'An Overview of the Music Therapy Literature Relating to Elderly People', in D. Aldridge (ed.), *Music Therapy in Dementia Care*. London: Jessica Kingsley. pp. 33–62.

Brown, D. and Peddar, J. (1991) *Introduction to Psychotherapy*. London: Routledge.

Brown, S. (1997) 'Supervision in Context: a balancing act', *British Journal of Music Therapy*, 11 (1): 4–12.

Brown, S. and Pavlicevic, M. (1996) 'Clinical Improvisation in Creative Music Therapy: musical aesthetic and the interpersonal dimension.' *The Arts in Psychotherapy*, 23 (5): 397–406.

Bruscia, K. (1987) *Improvisational Models of Music Therapy*. Springfield, IL: Charles C. Thomas.

Bruscia, K. (1998) *Defining Music Therapy*. Gilsum, NH: Barcelona.

Bruscia, K. (ed.) (1998) *The Dynamics of Music Psychotherapy*. Gilsum, NH: Barcelona.

BSMT (1968) 'Pioneers in Music Therapy', *British Society for Music Therapy, Bulletin*, 25: 17–19.

BSMT (2000) Information Booklet, British Society for Music Therapy.

Bunt, L. (1994) *Music Therapy: An Art Beyond Words*. London: Routledge.

Bunt, L., Burns, S. and Turton, P. (2000) 'Variations on a Theme: The Evolution of a Music Therapy Research Programme at the Bristol Cancer Help Centre', *British Journal of Music Therapy*, 14 (2): 56–69.

Cage, J. (1958) 'The Future of Music: Credo', in *Silence, Lectures and Writings by John Cage* (1987). London: Marion Boyars.

Casement, P. (1985) *On Learning from the Patient*. London: Routledge.

Committee of Enquiry into the Education of Handicapped Children and Young People (1978) *Special Educational Needs*. (The Warnock Report) London: HMSO.

Darnley-Smith, R. (1989) *Therapeutic Music and Music Therapy in Social Services Day Centre*. Unpublished document.

Darnley-Smith, R. (In Press) 'Psychodynamic Music Therapy in the Care of Older Adults', in S. Evans and J. Garner (eds), *Talking over the Years: A Handbook of Psychoanalytic Psychotherapy with Older People*. London: Routledge.

Davis, G. and Magee, W. (2001) 'Clinical Improvisation within Neurological Disease', *British Journal of Music Therapy*, 15 (2): 51–60.

Department of Health White Paper (2001) *Valuing People: A new Strategy for Learning Disability for the 21st Century*. London: The Department of Health, www.doh.gov.uk

Dileo, C. (2001) 'Ethical Issues in Supervision', in M. Forinash (ed.), *Music Therapy Supervision*. Gilsum, NH: Barcelona. pp. 19–38.

Dobbs, J. (1968) Chairman's Report, Annual General Meeting 1967, *British Society for Music Therapy, Bulletin* 25.

Dobbs, J.P.D. (1966) 'A Talk on The Work Of The Society', *British Society for Music Therapy, Bulletin* 21.

Dunbar, N. (2001) 'Groupwork in Creative Music Therapy: An Investigation into How Therapists Structure Musical Activities.' MMT dissertation, City University, London.

Flower, C. (1993) 'Control and Creativity', in M. Heal and T. Wigram (eds) *Music Therapy in Health and Education*. London: Jessica Kingsley. pp. 40–45.

Fry, D. (1962) 'Sound and Psychology', talk given to the Society of Music Therapy and Remedial Music, BSMT Archives.

Gale, C. (2000) *Key Dates in the development of music therapy in Wales*. Unpublished personal communication.

Gilroy, A. and Lee, C. (eds) (1995) *Art and Music Therapy and Research*. London: Routledge.

Goldberg, F.S. (1995) 'The Bonny Method of Guided Imagery and Music', in T. Wigram, B. Saperston and R. West (eds), *The Art and Science of Music Therapy: A Handbook*. Amsterdam: Harwood.

Gouk, P. (ed.) (2000) *Musical Healing in Cultural Contexts*. Aldershot: Ashgate.

Graham, J. (2000) 'Habitual Noise or Communication? Vocal Work in Music Therapy with Adults with Severe Learning Disability who make "Antisocial" Sounds'. MMT dissertation, City University, London.

Gray, A. (1994) *An Introduction to the Therapeutic Frame*. London and New York: Routledge.

Gregory, A.H. (1997) 'The Roles of Music in Society: the ethnomusicological perspective', in D. Hargreaves and A. North (eds), *The Social Psychology of Music*. Oxford: Oxford University Press. pp. 123–40.

Hadley, S. (2001) 'Exploring Relationships Between Mary Priestley's Life and Work', *Nordic Journal*, 10 (2): 116–31.

Hare, D. (1988) *Paris By Night*. London: Faber and Faber.

Hargreaves, D.J. and North, A.C. (eds) (1997) 'The Social Psychology of Music', in *The Social Psychology of Music*. Oxford: Oxford University Press. pp. 1–21.

Heal, M. (1989) 'The Use of Pre-composed Songs with a Highly Defended Client', *Journal of British Music Therapy*, 3 (1): 10–15.

Heal, M. (1994) 'The Development of Symbolic Function in a Young Woman with Down's Syndrome', in D. Dokter (ed.), *Arts Therapies and Clients with Eating Disorders*. London: Jessica Kingsley. pp. 279–94.

Heal, M., and Wigram, T. (eds) (1993) *Music Therapy in Health and Education*. London: Jessica Kingsley.

Hoad, T.F. (ed.) (1996) *Concise Dictionary of English Etymology*. Oxford: Oxford University Press.

Hooper, J. (2001) 'An Introduction to Vibroacoustic Therapy and an Examination of its Place in Music Therapy Practice', *British Journal of Music Therapy*, 15 (2): 69–77.

Horden, P. (ed.) (2000) 'Introduction', in *Music as Medicine*. Aldershot: Ashgate. pp. 1–3.

Hoskyns (1995) 'Observing Offenders: The Use of Simple Rating Scales to Assess Changes in Activity During Group Music Therapy', in A. Gilroy and C. Lee (eds), *Art and Music Therapy and Research*. London: Routledge. pp. 138–51.

Howes, F. (1962) 'Rhythm And Man', talk given to the Society of Music Therapy and Remedial Music, BSMT Archives.

Ibberson, C. (1996) 'A Natural End: One Story about Catherine', *British Journal of Music Therapy*, 10 (1): 24–31.

John, D. (1992) 'Towards Music Psychotherapy', *Journal of British Music Therapy*, 6 (1): 10–1.

John, D. (1995) 'The Therapeutic Relationship in Music Therapy as a Tool in the Treatment of Psychosis', in T. Wigram, B. Saperston and R. West (eds), *The Art and Science of Music Therapy: A Handbook.* Amsterdam: Harwood. pp. 157–66.

Johnson, M. (1966) 'Conference Report', *Society for Music Therapy and Remedial Music Bulletin,* 21: 3–14.

Jung, C.F. (1972) *Four Archetypes – Mother, Rebirth, Spirit, Trickster.* London: Routledge & Kegan Paul.

Kalsched, D. (1996) *The Inner World of Trauma – Archetypal Defenses of the Personal Spirit.* London and New York: Routledge.

Laing, R.D. (1986) *The Divided Self.* Harmondsworth: Pelican. (1st Edition: 1960: Tavistock Publications.)

Lee, C. (1995) 'The Analysis of Therapeutic Improvisatory Music', in A. Gilroy and C. Lee (eds), *Art and Music Therapy and Research.* London: Routledge. pp. 35–50.

Levinge, A. (1993) 'Permission to Play. The Search for the Self Through Music Therapy Research with Children Presenting Communication Difficulties', in H. Payne (ed.), *Handbook of Inquiry in the Arts Therapies.* London: Jessica Kingsley. pp. 218–28.

Levinge, A. (1999) PhD dissertation, University of Birmingham: Birmingham.

Lloyd, G.E.R. (ed.) (1986) *Hippocratic Writings.* Harmondsworth: Penguin.

Loth, H. (2000) 'Historical Perspectives Interview Series: Tony Wigram interviewed by Helen Loth', *British Journal of Music Therapy,* 14 (1): 5–12.

Madsen, C.K., Cotter, V. and Madsen, C.H., Jr. (1968) 'A Behavioral Approach to Music Therapy', *Journal of Music Therapy,* 5 (3): 69–71.

Madsen, C.K. and Madsen, C.H., Jr. (1968) 'Music as a Behavior Modification Technique with a Juvenile Delinquent' *Journal of Music Therapy,* 5 (3): 72–76. Reprinted in J.H. Standley and C.A. Prickett (eds) (1994) *Research in Music Therapy: A Tradition of Excellence. Outstanding Reprints from the Journal of Music Therapy.* Silver Spring, MD: National Association for Music Therapy. pp. 585–90.

Malloch, S. (1999) *Mothers and Infants and Communicative Musicality. Special Issue of Musicae Scientiae*: Rhythm, Musical Narrative and Origins of Human Communication, pp. 29–57. Trevarthen amd Malloch (2000).

Milner, M. (1952) 'Aspects of Symbolism and Comprehension of the Not-self', *International Journal of Psycho-analysis* 33: 181–95. Cited in Gray (1994), p. 5.

Montague, S. (1998) Programme note for Musicircus by John Cage. London: Barbican Centre.

Moss, H. (1999) 'Creating a New Music Therapy Post: An Evidence Based Research Project', *British Journal of Music Therapy,* 13 (2): 49–58.

Nordoff, P. (1976) Interview for BBC television programme *Parents and Children.*

Nordoff, P. and Robbins, C. (1977) *Creative Music Therapy.* New York: John Day. (Out of print. New revised edition forthcoming). Gilsum, NH: Barcelona.

Nordoff, P. and Robbins, C. (1992) *Therapy in Music for Handicapped Children.* (1st edn 1971). London: Gollancz.

Odell-Miller, H. (1991) 'Group Improvisation Therapy: The Experience of One Man with Schizophrenia', in K.E. Bruscia (ed.), *Case Studies in Music Therapy.* Phoenixville, PN: Barcelona.

Odell-Miller, H. (1995) 'Why Provide Music Therapy in the Community for Adults with Mental Health Problems', *British Journal of Music Therapy,* 9 (1): 4–10.

Oldfield, A. and Adams, M. (1995) 'The Effect of Music Therapy on a Group of Adults with Profound Learning Difficulties', in A. Gilroy and C. Lee (eds), *Art and Music Therapy and Research*. London: Routledge. pp. 164–82.

Oldfield, A. and Bunce, L. (2001) 'Mummy Can Play Too ... Short-term Music Therapy with Mothers and Young Children', *British Journal of Music Therapy*, 15 (1): 27–36.

Pavlicevic, M. (1990) 'Dynamic Interplay in Clinical Improvisation', *Journal of British Music Therapy*, 4 (2): 5–9.

Pavlicevic, M. (1995) 'Music and Emotion: Aspects of Music Therapy Research', in A. Gilroy and C. Lee (eds), *Art And Music: Therapy And Research*. London: Routledge. pp. 51–65.

Pavlicevic, M. (1997) *Music Therapy in Context: Music, Meaning and Relationship*. London: Jessica Kingsley.

Pavlicevic, M. (1999) 'New Beginnings and New Endings', *South African Journal of Music Therapy*, 17- 1999: 25–26.

Pavlicevic, M. (2001) 'A Child in Time and Health – Guiding Images in Music Therapy', *British Journal of Music Therapy*, 15 (1): 14–21.

Payne, H. (ed.) (1993) *Handbook of Inquiry in the Arts Therapies*. London: Jessica Kingsley.

Plato (1987) *The Republic*. Translated by D. Lee. Harmondsworth: Penguin.

Priestley, M. (1975) *Music Therapy in Action*. London: Constable.

Priestley, M. (1995) 'Linking Sound and Symbol', in T. Wigram, B. Saperston and R. West (eds), *The Art and Science of Music Therapy: A Handbook*. Amsterdam: Harwood.

Purdie, H. (1997) 'Music Therapy with Adults who have Traumatic Brain Injury and Stroke', *British Journal of Music Therapy*, 11 (2): 45–50.

Robarts, J. (1994) 'Towards Autonomy and a Sense of Self', in D. Dokter (ed.), *Arts Therapies and Clients with Eating Disorders*. London: Jessica Kingsley.

Robarts, J.Z. (1998) 'Music Therapy and Children With Autism', in C. Trevarthan, K. Aitken, D. Papoudi and J.Z. Robarts (eds), *Children With Autism: Diagnosis and Interventions to Meet Their Needs*. London: Jessica Kingsley. pp. 172–202.

Robertson, J. (1996) Appendix, unpublished minutes of Scottish Music Therapy Council Seminar, 14 September 1996.

Rogers, P.J. (1992) 'Issues in Child Sexual Abuse', *Journal of British Music Therapy*, 7 (2): 5–15.

Rogers, P. (1993) 'Research in Music Therapy with Sexually Abused Clients', in H. Payne (ed.), *Handbook of Inquiry in the Arts Therapies*. London: Jessica Kingsley. pp. 197–217.

Rowan, J. (1991) *The Reality Game*. London and New York: Routledge. (1st edn. 1983)

Rowling, J.K. (1997) *Harry Potter and the Philosopher's Stone*. London: Bloomsbury.

Scheiby, B.B. (1998) 'The Role of Musical Countertransference in Analytical Music Therapy', in K.E. Bruscia (ed.), *The Dynamics of Music Psychotherapy*. Gilsum, NH: Barcelona. pp. 213–47.

Scheiby, B.B. and Nygaard Pederson, I. (1999) *Nordic Journal of Music Therapy*, 8 (1): 58–71.

Schullian, D.M. and Schoen, M. (eds) (1948) *Music and Medicine*. New York: Schuman.

Sekeles, C. (1996) *Music: Motion and Emotion*. St Louis, MD: MMB Music.

Simpson, F. (2000) 'Speaking with Clients – Perspectives from Creative Music Therapy', *British Journal of Music Therapy*, 14 (2): 83–92.

Sinason, V. (1992) *Mental Handicap and the Human Condition – New Approaches from the Tavistock.* London: Free Association Books.

Skille, O. and Wigram, T. (1995) 'The Effects of Music Vocalisation and Vibration on Brain and Muscle Tissue: Studies in Vibroacoustic Therapy', in T. Wigram, B. Saperston and R. West (eds), *The Art and Science of Music Therapy: A Handbook.* Amsterdam: Harwood. pp. 23–57.

Sloboda, A. (1994) 'Individual Music Therapy with Anorexic and Bulimic Patients', in D. Dockter (ed.), *Arts Therapies and Clients with Eating Disorders.* London: Jessica Kingsley.

Sloboda, J. (1985) *The Musical Mind.* Oxford: Oxford Science Publications.

Standley, J. (1995) 'Music as a Therapeutic Intervention in Medical and Dental Treatment: Research and Clinical Applications', in T. Wigram, B. Saperston and R. West (eds), *The Art and Science of Music Therapy: A Handbook.* Amsterdam: Harwood. pp. 3–22.

Stern, D. (1985) The *Interpersonal World of the Infant: A View from Psychanalysis and Developmental Psychology.* New York: Basic Book.

Stewart, D. (2000) 'The State of the UK Music Therapy Profession: Personal Qualities, Working Models, Support Networks and Job Satisfaction', *British Journal of Music Therapy*, 14 (1): 13–27.

Stokes, J. and Sinason, V. (1992) 'Secondary Mental Handicap as a Defence', in A. Waitman and S. Conboy-Hill (eds), *'Psychotherapy and Mental Handicap'.* London: Sage.

Storr, A. (1992) *Music and The Mind.* London: Harper Collins.

Streeter, E. (1999) 'Finding a Balance between Psychological Thinking and Musical Awareness in Music Therapy Theory – a Psychoanalytic Perspective', *British Journal of Music Therapy*, 13 (1): 5–20.

Sutton J.P. (1995) 'The Sound-world of Speech and Language Impaired Children', in A. Gilroy and C. Lee (eds), *Art and Music Therapy and Research.* London: Routledge. pp. 152–63.

Sutton, J.P. (2000) *A Short History of Music Therapy in Northern Ireland,* unpublished paper.

Sutton, J.P. (2001) 'The Invisible Handshake: An Investigation of Free Musical Improvisation as a Form of Conversation'. PhD dissertation. Ulster: University of Ulster.

Sutton, J.P. (2002) 'Trauma in Context' in J.P. Sutton (ed.), *Music, Music Therapy and Trauma: International Perspectives.* London: Jessica Kingsley.

Swiller, H.I., Lang, E.A. and Halperin, D.A. (1993) 'Process Groups for Training Psychiatric Residents', in A. Alonso and H.I. Swiller (eds), *Group Therapy in Clinical Practice.* Washington, DC: American Psychiatric Press. pp. 533–45.

Trevarthen, C. and Malloch, S. (2000) 'The Dance of Wellbeing: Defining The Musical Therapeutic Effect', *Nordic Journal of Music Therapy*, 9 (2): 3–17.

Turry, A. (1998) 'Transference and countertransference in Nordoff–Robbins Music Therapy', in K. Bruscia (ed.), *The Dynamics of Music Psychotherapy.* Gilsum, NH: Barcelona. pp. 161–212.

Tustin, F. (1972) *Autism and Child Psychosis.* London: Hogarth.

Tyler, H.M. (1998) 'Behind the Mask – An Exploration of the True and False Self as revealed in Music Therapy', *British Journal of Music Therapy*, 12 (2): 60–66.

Tyler, H.M. (2000) 'The Music Therapy Profession in Modern Britain', in P. Horden (ed.), *Music as Medicine*. Aldershot: Ashgate.

Tyler, H. (2002) 'In the Music Prison' in J. Sutton (ed.) *Music, Music Therapy and Trauma: International Perspectives*. London: Jessica Kingsley.

Usher, J. (1998) 'Lighting up the Mind, Evolving a Model of Consciousness and Its Application to Improvisation in Music Therapy', *British Journal of Music Therapy*, 12 (1): 4–19.

Van Colle, S. and Williams, T. (1995) 'Starting Out in Music Therapy Process Research', in A. Gilroy and C. Lee (eds), *Art and Music Therapy and Research*. London: Routledge. pp. 85–100.

Vink, A. (2000) 'The Problem of Agitation in Elderly People and The Potential Benefit of Music Therapy', in D. Aldridge (ed.), *Music Therapy in Dementia Care*. London: Jessica Kingsley. pp. 102–118.

Weinreb, B. and Hibbert, C. (eds) (1983) *The London Encyclopaedia*. London: Macmillan.

West, M. (2000) 'Music Therapy in Antiquity', in P. Horden (ed.), *Music as Medicine*. Aldershot: Ashgate. pp. 51–68.

Wigram, T. (1993a) 'The Feeling of Sound. The Effect of Music and Low Frequency Sound in Reducing Anxiety and Challenging Behaviour in Clients with Learning Difficulties', in H. Payne (ed.), *Handbook of Inquiry in the Arts Therapies*. London: Jessica Kingsley. pp. 177–96.

Wigram, T. (1993b) 'Music Therapy Research', in M. Heal and T. Wigram (eds), *Music Therapy In Health And Education*. London: Jessica Kingsley.

Wigram, T. (1999) 'Contact in Music', in T. Wigram and J. De Backer (eds), *Clinical Applications of Music Therapy in Developmental Disability, Paediatrics and Neurology*. London: Jessica Kingsley.

Wigram, T., Rogers, P. and Odell-Miller, H. (1993) 'Music Therapy in the United Kingdom', in C. Dileo Maranto (ed.), *Music Therapy: International Perspectives*. Pipersville, PA: Jeffrey Books. pp. 573–604.

Wing, L. and Gould, J. (1979) 'Severe Impairments of Social Interactions and Associated Abnormalities in Children: Epidemiology and Classification', *Journal of Autism and Atypical Developmental Disorder*, 9: 11–29.

Winnicott, D.W. (1986) *Playing and Reality*. Harmondsworth: Penguin. (1st edn 1971).

Winnicott, D.W. (1990) 'Ego Distortion in Terms of the True and False Self', in *The Maturational Processes and the Facilitating Environment*. London: Karnac. (1st edn London: Hogarth 1965) pp. 140–152.

World Federation of Music Therapy, Bulletin 1, July 1997.

Zinkin, L. (1994) 'All's Well That End's Well. Or is it?', *Group Analysis*, 27 (1): 15–24.

INDEX